Praise for ~~~~

Weaving their very different experiences together with the threads of fresh spiritual insights and the wisdom of tradition, the authors of *Birthed in Prayer* have created a unique tapestry that women will cherish. Full of humorous, painful, and poignant observations, *Birthed in Prayer* prompts the reader to reflect on all the graced and gritty aspects of that most mysterious and miraculous of processes, pregnancy.

—Wendy M. Wright, PhD
Author of *Sacred Dwelling: A Spirituality of Family Life*
and *Seasons of a Family's Life: Cultivating
the Contemplative Spirit at Home*

Birthed in Prayer allows readers to explore more deeply the spiritual, emotional, and physical aspects of the profound changes occurring in their bodies. The authors share their own journeys of pregnancy and the journeys of other women they interviewed with such frankness and humility that each reader will feel free to express and explore her own fears, doubts, joys, worries, awe, and wonder at this time of her life. The insightful questions, journal suggestions, and personal exercises give structure to this exploration. And always the authors remind readers that their journey is in God's keeping, sustained by God's love and filled with divine presence.

—Patricia Wilson
Author of *Quiet Spaces: Prayer Interludes for Women*
and *When You Come Unglued, Stick Close to God*

Pregnancy, like the spiritual life, involves growth that leads to change. Expectant mothers (and fathers) can take this book as a companion on the journey to both parenthood and a deeper relationship with God. Readers will grow in their faith journey as they explore different women's personal experiences of pregnancy, scripture passages, questions for reflection, and suggested spiritual exercises. Among the assorted self-help books on pregnancy, *Birthed in Prayer* stands out with a focus on how the Creator is made known through pregnancy, and how a precious nine months can provide spiritual growth.

—Anne Broyles
Author of *Journaling: A Spiritual Journey* and *Priscilla and the Hollyhocks*

Birthed in Prayer is a much-needed gift for expectant mothers. Too often mothers-to-be prepare outwardly and tangibly for the coming changes in their lives without considering the necessary and inevitable inward changes. Kim Barker, Linda de Meillon, and Leigh Harrison guide readers on the spiritual journey of pregnancy by encouraging them to nourish their relationship with God—to look inward and pay attention spiritually to all that is transpiring in this nine-month journey. By using personal stories, thought-provoking quotations, pertinent scriptures, journaling ideas, reflection questions, and prayers, the authors skillfully lead readers to encounter God in a new way during this time of holy waiting.

—Betty Shannon Cloyd
Author of *Children and Prayer*
and *Parents and Grandparents as Spiritual Guides*

Birthed in Prayer presents a frank, engaging, and unremittingly hopeful testimony to grace. This is a celebratory book, an inspired guide that presents pregnancy as "an invitation to wholeness." What better context can there be for "living forward"—for being deliberate disciples willing to grow in purposeful faith?

—Derek Maul, columnist for the *Tampa Tribune*
Author of *Get Real: A Spiritual Journey for Men*

Birthed in Prayer

Pregnancy as a Spiritual Journey

Kim Barker, Linda de Meillon, Leigh Harrison

UPPER
ROOM BOOKS®
NASHVILLE

Birthed in Prayer: Pregnancy as a Spiritual Journey
Copyright © 2008 by Kim Barker, Linda de Meillon, and Leigh Harrison
All rights reserved.

UPPER ROOM®, UPPER ROOM BOOKS®, and design logos are trademarks owned by The Upper Room®, a Ministry of GBOD®, Nashville, Tennessee. All rights reserved.

The Upper Room Web site: www.upperroom.org

This book was originally published as *Birthed in Prayer* © 2006, by Kim Barker, Leigh Harrison, and Linda de Meillon, by Struik Christian Books. A division of New Holland Publishing (South Africa) (Pty) Ltd., 80 McKenzie Street, Cape Town 8001, South Africa.

Scripture quotations designated NRSV are from the New Revised Standard Version Bible, copyright 1989, Division of Christian Education of the National Council of the Churches of Christ in the United States of America. Used by permission. All rights reserved. Scripture quotations designated NIV are from the HOLY BIBLE, NEW INTERNATIONAL VERSION®. Copyright © 1973, 1978, 1984 by International Bible Society. Used by permission of Zondervan. All rights reserved. Scripture quotations designated NLT are taken from the *Holy Bible, New Living Translation*, copyright © 1996. Used by permission of Tyndale House Publishers, Inc., Wheaton, Illinois 60189. All rights reserved. Scripture quotations designated GNT are taken from the GOOD NEWS TRANSLATION, SECOND EDITION. Copyright © 1992 by American Bible Society. Used by permission. All rights reserved. Scripture quotations designated *The Message* are taken from *The Message* by Eugene H. Peterson, copyright © 1993, 1994, 1995, 1996, 2000, 2001, 2002. Used by permission of NavPress Publishing Group. All rights reserved.

At the time of publication all Web sites referenced in this book were valid. However, due to the fluid nature of the Internet, some addresses may have changed or the content may no longer be relevant.

Excerpts from *Sacred Journeys: A Woman's Book of Daily Prayer*. Copyright © 1995 by Jan L. Richardson. Used by permission of the author. www.janrichardson.com

Cover image: © Jose Luis Pelaez, Inc. / CORBIS

Cover and interior design: Buckinghorse Design / www.buckinghorsedesign.com

First printing: 2008

LIBRARY OF CONGRESS CATALOGING-IN-PUBLICATION DATA

Barker, Kim.
    Birthed in prayer : pregnancy as a spiritual journey / Kim Barker, Linda de Meillon, Leigh Harrison.
        p. cm.
    Includes bibliographical references.
ISBN 978-0-8358-9941-3
1. Pregnant women—Religious life. 2. Pregnancy—Religious aspects—Christianity. I. De Meillon, Linda. II. Harrison, Leigh. III. Title.
BV4529.18.B35 2007
248.8'431—dc22   2007029991

Printed in the United States of America

To our daughters:
Shervon, Alyssa, Sinead, Caydn, and Kelby

CONTENTS

ACKNOWLEDGMENTS

Writing this book has been like a pregnancy, only much longer. Many people have been involved along the way to whom we would like to extend our heartfelt thanks.

First, we want to thank the women who shared their pregnancy stories with us through questionnaires and conversations—we are deeply grateful for your courage and generosity. Your stories breathed life into the dry bones of our ideas.

A huge bouquet of thanks goes to our families and friends who read early drafts, encouraged and supported us, and stepped in to help at various times in various ways. In particular we want to thank Chris, Shervon, Alyssa, Francois, Sinead, Dave, Caydn, and Kelby for believing in us and in this project and for releasing us each in our own way to complete this book.

We also extend our deep gratitude to Upper Room Books and to the editorial team there that nurtured our book with as much care and sensitivity as we did. It has been a privilege to work with you all.

Finally, we want to say how much we have appreciated the creative, dynamic process that the writing of this book became. It was both a privilege and a challenge to bring together three unique styles and personalities and to allow each person to have a voice while forging a united vision and purpose for the book. We gained so much from one another in the process, and our spiritual lives were deeply enriched by the experience.

INTRODUCTION

Linda, Leigh, and I wrote this book because it's the kind of book we would have liked to read when we were pregnant. We are all keen readers, and we consulted many books during our nine months as moms-to-be. We followed our babies' developments in utero through beautifully illustrated articles, books, and Web sites. We read about what to eat and how to exercise. We read about birth options and all the preparations we needed to make for our babies' arrivals. But something was missing.

Nobody was writing about the spirituality of pregnancy. We could not find any books that spoke to us as women of faith caught up in this overwhelming life experience. We also discovered that many thoughts and feelings we were having were never mentioned. Most pregnancy books glossed over uncomfortable emotions and ignored spiritual questions altogether. Books on faith and spirituality offered valuable insights, but we longed for those insights to be applied to pregnancy. There seemed to be an empty space on bookstore shelves, waiting for a book that addressed the emotional and spiritual needs of pregnant women in an honest and helpful way. We decided to write that book.

Pregnancy as a Time of Transition

Pregnancy is life-changing. A positive pregnancy test heralds the beginning of a new chapter of our lives, whether we are first-time moms or the mothers of two, three, or even more children. From the moment we know we are pregnant, we enter a time of transition—a time of waiting and preparing as we anticipate the arrival of the new little person who will share our lives.

We believe that pregnancy can be a God-given "stopping point"—an opportunity to reflect on our lives, values, and relationships; to reevaluate our choices and priorities; and to make some adjustments. Even more importantly, pregnancy can offer an occasion to draw closer to God and encounter God in a new way.

We hope this book will become a treasured companion for your pregnancy and beyond. We want to offer you a safe place to acknowledge honestly your thoughts and feelings and to spend time in prayerful reflection. We pray that this book will be a resource for your inner journey and that it will help you make meaning of your pregnancy in a way that is healing, hope-filled, and life-giving.

This book does not focus on preparing you for having a baby. Rather, it invites you on a journey of awareness and growth as you prepare for motherhood. Pregnancy is one of many life transitions, and we would like this book to partner with you through this time of change so that you feel more prepared for other changes that lie ahead. We hope the invitations to reflection and prayer will encourage you to build a strong foundation of spiritual practice that will help you stand firm and grow through all of life, not just during your pregnancy.

Birthing a Book

This book was conceived and written in community. It was our first time to work this way or to write this kind of book. Because we live in different cities in South Africa, we first met to discuss ideas about the book over coffee in a One-Stop Wimpy, a fast-food restaurant about the same distance from each of our homes. That morning we discovered that we could not speak about pregnancy in abstract terms. Whichever direction the discussion took, we ended up telling a story about our own pregnancies.

We realized that we shared a passion for stories and their power to connect people on an emotional level. And we knew that we wanted to reach the hearts of women through this book, so we began writing our own pregnancy stories.

As we wrote and shared, we became increasingly curious about other women's pregnancy stories. We found ourselves chatting to the women we knew about their pregnancies, and their responsiveness amazed us. Women seemed so eager to talk about their pregnancies, and we often heard the words, "You know, I have never spoken about this before, but . . ."

We decided to create a questionnaire that would invite women to share their stories in a more formal way so that we could include them in the book. We put together a simple set of questions and sent them to friends, family members, and work colleagues, explaining our ideas for the book and asking them to share their own stories about pregnancy.

The questionnaire evolved a bit over time, but these were the key questions we asked:

- How many pregnancies have you had?
- How did you react each time you found out you were pregnant?
- What was the most positive aspect of your pregnancy(ies)?
- What was the most negative?
- What surprised you the most about pregnancy?
- What do you wish you had known before becoming pregnant?
- In what ways did you experience God during your pregnancy(ies)?
- How did your pregnancy(ies) affect your relationship with others?
- How did your pregnancy(ies) affect your sense of self?

We invited women to write as much or as little as they wished in response to each question and to feel free to add any other information that was meaningful or important to them, even if it didn't fit these questions.

As the questionnaires began to come in and we read the stories, we realized that we were standing on holy ground. Women shared openly and honestly, and their stories reflected a range of emotions from pain, confusion, isolation, fear, and anger to joy, serenity, excitement, awe, wonder, and acceptance. We handled the stories with reverence and spent many hours reading them aloud to one another, weeping at times and laughing at times. We prayed for each woman who had shared her story, and for her family. These were rich and precious mornings.

Next we developed a vision statement and planned the book's structure and content. We made a key commitment in approaching our writing: we would resist the temptation to sound like experts on pregnancy. We are not experts. We are simply three women on a journey that has encompassed pregnancy and motherhood, sharing our thoughts and stories (as well as a few of our more acceptable neuroses) with other women. And although the book has changed since those early days, all along we were guided by our original vision statement and kept coming back to it when we went off on a tangent:

Our purpose in writing this book is to nourish the inner being of those experiencing pregnancy, especially in their relationship with God.

We met to discuss and plan the chapters and divided the chapters among us to write. We didn't try to sound the same, and we each brought a distinctive style and emphasis to our chapters, allowing our own stories to guide and shape our writing. Later we had the opportunity to read and give feedback on one another's work (a learning process all its own), as well as to edit each other's chapters. So, in the end there is a little of each of us in every chapter.

However, we have indicated who wrote each chapter and hope that you enjoy getting to know us each a bit better as you come to recognize our distinctive styles and hear our stories. But we also hope that you will sense a deep resonance among chapters in our approach to God, spirituality, life, and, most of all, pregnancy.

At this point we need to apologize to all dads-in-waiting who are looking for a book like this one to address *their* journey through the pregnancy. We do not consider a father's role any less important than a mother's, but we have no experience in being fathers, expectant or otherwise. When we decided that the book would be rooted in and shaped by our own stories as women, it became clear that this book would speak primarily to women. Having said that, we invite all dads-to-be to dip into the book as well, and we would be delighted if you find nourishment for your own journey. Perhaps you might be inspired to write a similar book for men.

We also need to say a word about gender and pronouns. Clearly all expectant mothers would be "she," so that one was easy, but babies could be boys or girls, so there we faced a choice. We have tried to be equitable between the "he's" and "she's," but gender references may be skewed by our own experiences. Among us we have five daughters and no sons, so if we have erred on the side of emphasizing the feminine when we refer to babies, it is simply because it is all we know. Also, we chose to use inclusive language for God, but many of the women's stories and scripture passages refer to God in masculine terms, and we did not change these.

As we began to share our own pregnancy stories over coffee in the Wimpy more than three years ago, none of us could have anticipated how both the book and our relationships would grow and mature or how long the writing process would take! We have often felt that writing this book has been a bit like a pregnancy itself and feel rather maternal as we launch our little one out into the big, wide world. This book was conceived and nurtured in prayer—our own and the prayers of those close to us, and we continue to pray as we send it out to accomplish whatever our gracious and loving God has in mind for it.

As you begin reading this book, know that you were prayed for before one word of the book was written, and you are still prayed for now. May that knowledge enfold you, warm you, and delight you as you journey through each chapter.

Introducing Ourselves

Linda

I am married to Francois, and we have a nearly eight-year-old daughter, Sinead. When Sinead was a year old, I decided to leave my career in teacher training to spend more time with her. I believe that motherhood is the hardest job I've ever held, but the rewards far outweigh anything I did before. While I was at home, God challenged me to explore my passion for writing, so another adventure was birthed in my life. I feel honored and privileged to be writing my first book on such a life-changing experience as pregnancy.

In between the often frenetic bouts of writing and mothering, I am involved in my church's preschool ministry, dance and drama, and a cell group (small group for spiritual growth and accountability). I also present creativity workshops for Christian women and offer support and trauma debriefing at my local police station.

Kim

I grew up in a household of boys; I was the only girl, with an older and a younger brother. What a difference from my family now, where my husband, Dave, is totally outnumbered by the women in the house—even the hamster is a girl, we think!

My two daughters—Caydn, age eight, and Kelby, age six—are a source of joy and delight and my ever-present reminder that I need to keep growing. They push all my buttons, good and bad, and I am eternally grateful that they are around to do that.

I originally qualified as a speech and hearing therapist, but my work and academic life has meandered through peacekeeping, applied linguistics, developing educational materials, research, editing, and writing. More recently I completed studies in pastoral therapy and have discovered a passion for facilitating groups, workshops, and retreats.

Leigh

I grew up in Zimbabwe with my parents, three sisters, and then much later a brother. I met my husband, Christopher, at Rhodes University in Grahamstown. We have two teenage daughters, Shervon and Alyssa, and thrive on the joys and challenges of parenting two outspoken, dynamic young people in the twenty-first century. We have a family mission statement that speaks of our commitment to honor God, care for others and ourselves, work together, and very importantly, make time for fun and adventure.

I have always worked in some form of personal development, from rural community leadership development to spiritual awareness and growth to performance training. I juggle my time running my business, supporting my family, and more recently and most exciting, writing this book. I love going out for breakfast with my husband, laughing with my girls, and discovering new and wonderful places.

Suggestions for Using This Book

You can approach this book in many ways. See it as an open door—you are welcome to enter at any time, stay for as long as you wish, and leave whenever you are ready. The book is an invitation rather than a prescription, so there is no set way to use it.

You may want to work through the book on your own, starting with any chapter that appeals particularly to you. The structure of the book is fairly open; feel free to dip in at any point.

Every chapter is punctuated by regular stopping points we have called Reflection. The Reflection sections contain questions to help you think about what you have read in light of your own experience. You may spend a few minutes on a question, or you may need to think about it for days. We encourage you to record your thoughts and responses in a journal and to stay with each question for as long as necessary.

Each chapter ends with a section called Invitation to Prayer. Each Invitation to Prayer guides you in prayer related to the content of the chapter. It provides an opportunity to bring all your thoughts and feelings to God. As you reach the end of each chapter, set aside some time to be quiet and focus on the Invitation to Prayer. Again, though, there is no pressure and no right or wrong way of doing it.

You might work through the book with another pregnant friend or even with a group of friends, perhaps from a prenatal class. The questions may then form the basis of sharing, support, and mutual prayer. And although the book is written with women in mind, you may find it helpful to work through it with your husband.

A Last Word Before We Begin

Perhaps more than anything else, through this book we want to invite you into the practice of paying attention. Pregnancy is a sacred time, a mystery, a holy business; but it is also very fleeting. When we pay attention to this awesome experience, we may somehow encounter the God at the center of it all, the God who breathes life into our wombs, the God who calls forth, who creates and shapes a new being out of the seed of our humanity.

Pregnancy is a sacred time, a mystery, a holy business; but it is also very fleeting.

This is the same God who created you and me, and who continues to shape and form us. As we encounter our Creator in our pregnancy, we realize that God is as interested in our lives and our growth as in the life and growth of our baby. So, this book is also about becoming aware of what is happening in our own lives and listening to our own inner voices as well as to the voice of God. God breathes life into our dry and barren places and calls us forth to live in freedom and to be all that we were created to be.

It takes courage to become aware. It takes courage to encounter and be encountered by God. And it takes courage to be a mother. But in doing so we open ourselves to experiencing the fullness of life. We invite you to join us on the journey.

What's in this chapter?

*T*he discovery that you are pregnant is an awesome moment. This chapter invites you to take time to gather your thoughts, reflect on your response to the news, and bring all your thoughts and feelings to God.

We also recognize that you have embarked on a journey of change, and we relate the process of change to the structure of this book, providing a road map for the way forward through the chapters that follow.

- The pregnancy test was positive!
- Take time to catch your breath
- The journey ahead
- Invitation to Prayer: Beginning your journey with God

1

I'M PREGNANT!

Where did you come from, baby dear?
Out of the everywhere into the here.
—George MacDonald, *At the Back of the North Wind*

Linda . . .

Well, what do you think?" the doctor said, eyeing the slip of paper with what looked to me like gobbledygook on it. What did I think? To be honest, I wasn't allowing myself the luxury of thinking.

After suffering years of infertility and being subjected to countless maybes and what-ifs, I'd learned not to think much about the possibility of pregnancy so I wouldn't set myself up for the inevitable letdown. Anyway, I certainly hadn't come for a pregnancy test—the doctor had thrown that curveball. I'd come for a good dose of kill-or-cure for a chronic cough, and the doctor, upon learning that my period was four days late, insisted on a test before prescribing medication. I begged her not to put me through this, but eventually I emerged from the restroom, clutching the plastic cup, and sat impatiently, waiting for the little slip of paper that would confirm once again our inability to conceive.

"What I think," I began, "is that it's too soon to tell because I've been four days late before, and I've consumed copious amounts of cough syrup."

"Well, the test is positive."

"Oh. Um . . . positive for what?"

"Positive. You're pregnant."

It was an incredible moment, and I get emotional every time I relive it. My hands flew to my face; my doctor got up and hugged me and pressed the phone into my hands to call Francois, who was so overcome that he had to excuse himself from the office. Amid the whoops and shrieks, my blood tests were done and I drank gallons of water for a preliminary scan. All the while I kept asking, "Are you sure it's there?" I was convinced that someone was going to tell me it was a mistake.

For me, pregnancy felt like a completion, a destination reached at the end of the long and lonely road of infertility.

I remember wanting to gag from all the excitement. In an effort to behave in a calmer manner, I composed myself and asked, "So, what do you think will be the best thing for my cough?" which was met with screams of laughter.

I was sent packing with my prescription for folic acid and emerged into a rainy parking lot, where a parking attendant met me, umbrella in hand. My first impulse was to tell him my news, but then I thought better of it. I drove home in a fog. I had a shattering headache and still could not comprehend the enormity of what had just happened. When Francois came home, we hugged and cried as I relived the doctor's visit. It would be a tale I'd relive dozens of times: The Story of How I Went to the Doctor for a Cough and Came Back with a Baby. When Sinead was born, Francois remarked that her birth was the greatest day of his life—and I wouldn't want to diminish that—but finding out I was pregnant was the greatest day of mine.

For me, pregnancy felt like a completion, a destination finally reached at the end of the long, lonely road of infertility. It was the sweetest surprise, and my stunned reaction was overwhelmingly wonderful. Others may have similar feelings when a pregnancy is planned or long awaited. Even a surprise pregnancy can be a source of great joy when you realize it's something that you really want. This is how Elize described her response:

> I was very happy . . . I was so overcome. I believed that it was meant to be because we didn't plan the pregnancy, and I became pregnant while using the Pill.

But it is also true that many women feel ambivalent about a "positive" result. Perhaps you have been caught unawares, and the timing does not feel right. You may feel you're not ready because you haven't been married long, or your situation seems complicated and demanding and you wonder how a baby will fit in. Some women may feel concerned that their careers will be affected adversely, or perhaps they had assumed that their families were complete. Gayle initially experienced shock and uncertainty. She said:

> When I saw the test was positive, it kind of caught me off guard. We had to spend some time coming to terms with the fact that I was pregnant so quickly. Was it really God's timing for us to have a baby? Were we really ready? I was so surprised, and I had to tell myself that it was a good thing that I was pregnant!

Like Gayle, many of us just need a little time to get used to the idea.

Kim had been trying to get pregnant for years. Her reaction to finding out she was pregnant at last is perhaps typical of the strange conflict that plays out in our minds when we get the news. She described her feelings immediately after putting down the phone:

> I had imagined the joy, the excitement, and the sheer thrill of knowing that my body was able to conceive a child. But I had not anticipated the feeling that flooded over me only moments after I had put the phone down: *Oh my goodness. This is real. I'm going to have*

a baby, and everything will change. There's no turning back now. I was joyful and excited, wanting to dance and sing and hug the world. And I was absolutely terrified.

Some women may have even stronger feelings than ambivalence. What if you don't feel happy at all? What if you feel numb or even angry? What if your circumstances seem far from ideal? Unhappiness about being pregnant can be frightening. Bronwen and Lauren described their reactions to their second pregnancies:

> Christie was a total surprise. Because the pregnancy was unplanned and because I'd experienced a traumatic birth with my first baby and had had lots of complications, I was really upset. I just felt that I wasn't ready to go through another pregnancy.
>
> —Bronwen

> The pregnancy was unplanned. My experience of pregnancy hadn't been positive, and I didn't look forward to going through another period of discomfort and tiredness. I couldn't feel joy initially . . . After a while, when I'd given myself some time to work through it, the wonder and joy became apparent, and I saw it as a God-planned pregnancy.
>
> —Lauren

The stories of how we felt when we discovered our pregnancies will probably be etched into our memories forever. Certainly one's first pregnancy is a definitive moment in her life—a moment captured because it so clearly defines a "before" and an "after." In an instant, our sense of who we are shifts, yet there is little tangible that distinguishes us from the person we were before. We don't essentially change as women, but we acquire an additional role as mother-to-be, and somehow we know that our lives will never again be the same.

Leigh remembers looking in the mirror when she first heard that she was pregnant:

> I ran my hands over my tummy and wondered what it would look and feel like, round and full with a tiny baby hidden inside. I peered at my face and wondered if I looked different. I didn't, of course, although I felt that I should. Nothing had changed, and yet everything had.

Many of us will delight in our pregnancy and in the incredible privilege of bringing another human being into the world. But by its very nature, pregnancy represents radical change in every aspect of our lives. Even as we realize that we are pregnant, we may also realize some of the far-reaching implications of our pregnancy. It is not unusual to feel anxious about facing some of the difficulties and adjustments that accompany change. We all react to the changes associated with pregnancy in different ways depending on, among other things, our personality, the circumstances of our pregnancy, the quality of our relationships with people who will support us, and our connection to God.

However you responded to the news of your pregnancy, we pray that in this book you will find acceptance and understanding, as well as a safe place in which to explore your thoughts and feelings as you move through this time of transition into motherhood.

Reflection

How did you respond to discovering you were pregnant?

Take Time to Catch Your Breath

> Making the decision to have a child—it's momentous. It is to decide forever to have your heart go walking around outside your body.
>
> —Elizabeth Stone, *The Best of Women's Quotations*[1]

In the midst of all the excitement and fuss, it may help to stop for a moment and take a deep breath! Whether we're over the moon, feeling a mixture of anxiety and excitement, or still reeling from the shock, we need to take some time to gather our thoughts and reflect. How are we actually feeling? What does this all mean?

Maybe you're on an emotional high; I certainly was. I don't think I ever came down from the clouds all through my pregnancy, despite my gynecologist's concerns that I was an older mother and that certain dangers accompanied my age. I simply couldn't help basking in what I believed was truly a gift from God.

I often took time to reflect on what this joy meant to me. My relationship with God took on a new dimension.

I often took time to reflect on what this joy meant to me. My relationship with God took on a new dimension: I felt blessed, sought out, and special. I spent precious quiet times with God and praised God for God's faithfulness to us. Our pregnancy gave testimony to a miraculous God, and it encouraged others who were also trusting God for a breakthrough in their lives.

If we're dealing with uncertainty and wavering between emotions, it's important to acknowledge all our feelings and bring them to God. Recording our thoughts in a journal and sharing them with our husband or a trusted friend can also help. Talking about feelings of anxiety, doubt, or confusion can help us clear our heads and gain new perspective so that we can become more open to the possibilities that lie ahead. It can also help us get in touch with the courage and confidence we need to fulfill the new role into which God has called us.

Reflection

What are you feeling right now? If you find it helpful, write about your feelings in your journal.

The Journey Ahead

> Life is always changing; we are always changing. We live in a river of change, and a river of change lives within us.
> —Elizabeth Lesser, *Broken Open*[2]

As we have already mentioned, pregnancy is a time of unavoidable change and transition. Change always requires leaving behind the known and familiar in order to experience something new. Change is a process, a journey we undertake—whether willingly or unwillingly—that seems to involve three movements within our hearts, minds, and spirits.

The first movement entails saying good-bye to our familiar ways of being and doing. Letting go of the way things were before we became pregnant isn't easy, but it is necessary. What we do with our time, how we look, what draws our attention, how we are perceived, and how we relate to others will all change with our transition into motherhood. The challenge and invitation of pregnancy is to acknowledge what we are releasing and to allow ourselves to mourn our losses.

We talk about this first movement in the journey of change in chapters 2–4 ("Listening to Our Stories," "Releasing the Way Things Were," and "Recognizing Myths").

The second movement in the change process is actually more like standing still. It occurs in that in-between phase when we are no longer what we were before but have not yet fully moved into what we will be. We are in limbo. This is a time of waiting, receiving, and resting. It is also a time to confront honestly who we are and what we struggle with; a time when we need to make space in our hearts and minds to hear the still, small voice of God. It is an opportunity to "restore myself to myself" before I move into the next chapter of my life.

Chapters 5–8 ("Facing Fear," "Encountering God," "Becoming Whole," and "Waiting") relate to this in-between phase in our transition to motherhood.

The third movement on the change journey invites us to orient ourselves toward welcoming the new. Having released those things that we were holding on to, we can willingly embrace all that motherhood has to offer. We can welcome its opportunities and challenges, and we can welcome our baby with open arms.

We speak of various aspects of this third movement in chapters 9–10 ("Embracing Others" and "Preparing for What Will Be").

An exciting journey lies ahead, but for now, let's just draw aside and give ourselves some time and space as we contemplate this discovery of our pregnancy. As followers of Christ, we are invited to trust that God's timing is never wrong. The God who flung the stars into space and who sustains the earth, the God who clothes the lilies of the field and is mindful of the sparrows, is the One who ordains every season, appoints every sunset, and creates every new life.

Take a moment to think about the process of conception. It is nothing short of a miracle. Even though science has tried to analyze, explain, and even replicate this miracle, it is no less amazing. In many ways the mystery only deepens, as each new insight seems to lead to further questions. We just do not fully understand how two single cells can combine to create the one cell, which then divides and develops into a unique and complex living being.

Lewis Thomas writes that the mere existence of the cell created by the joining of a sperm and an egg "should be one of the greatest astonishments of the earth. People ought to be walking around all day, all through their waking hours, calling to each other in endless wonderment, talking of nothing except that cell."[3]

In many ways, as human knowledge has increased, we have become quite blasé about the mechanics of human reproduction. It seems so common, so natural, and surely so ordinary. But the moment of conception still remains beyond the grasp of human control. Margaret Hebblethwaite believes that:

> Choosing to have a baby is not simply within our power. We can open up that possibility, we can go a long way towards enabling it to happen, but we cannot dictate it. In the end it is God who gives life . . . we can be co-operators in God's creating, but not ourselves creators.[4]

Many times in this book we will come back to the story of Mary, the mother of Jesus. Hers is probably the most powerful account of conception, pregnancy, and birth the world has ever known. We first encounter Mary when an angel of God appears to her and tells her that God is about to conceive an extraordinary life within her, a baby who will be both human and divine. In light of her circumstances—a virgin promised in marriage to a man of good character and standing in the community—this was not necessarily good news.

Mary's culture would have shunned an unmarried pregnant girl, and she would have had to endure slander, rejection, and perhaps even death by stoning. Mary knew this, and I can't imagine that she didn't feel afraid.

But Mary's faith proves stronger than fear or uncertainty. She submits to the angel's message and trusts in the outcome. Now, if an angel rather than a blood test announced our pregnancy, we would probably find it easier to trust God that our baby's life has been called forth at this particular time for a particular purpose. But in the absence of a divine messenger, we will need to draw on the faith that has grown as we have walked with God, in order to say with Mary: "May it be to me as you have said" (Luke 1:38, NIV).

Reflection

- Bring your responses to your pregnancy to God. Tell God everything: your uncertainties, joys, fears, and appreciation.
- How might your pregnancy be affected by believing and trusting that God is the one who has given life to your baby at this particular time?

Invitation to Prayer

Read through the following scriptures a few times, slowly:

Did you not pour me out like milk
    and curdle me like cheese,
clothe me with skin and flesh
    and knit me together with bones and sinews?
You gave me life and showed me kindness,
    and in your providence watched over my spirit.

                       —Job 10:10-12, NIV

Before I was born the LORD called me;
    from my birth he has made mention of my name.

                       —Isaiah 49:1, NIV

Before I formed you in the womb I knew you,
before you were born I set you apart.

                       —Jeremiah 1:5, NIV

What do these scriptures mean to you? What is God saying to you about the way God planned and formed you? What is God saying about the way the Creator planned and is forming your baby? What in your heart right now would you like to share with God?

The ancient Israelites had a tradition of positioning a stone or a pillar of stones to mark a place where the divine presence had been revealed. Jacob did this after he dreamed of heaven opening, saw the stairway of angels, and heard God speaking to him (Gen. 28:10-22).

The pillar of stones became an ongoing reminder of God's goodness and faithfulness.

The discovery that you are pregnant is a special moment in which God can reveal God's self to you. You may wish also to mark this moment in a physical way that will always remind you of God's goodness and faithfulness. Perhaps you can put a large rock or pile of stones in a special place in your garden, or plant a tree that will grow just as your baby will grow in the weeks, months, and years to come.

You might plan to do this with your husband as part of a simple ceremony to mark this momentous time for you as a couple. Or you may choose to share the moment with a friend or family member.

Use the time you set aside to thank God for the precious gift entrusted to you. Invite God to walk with you and your husband on your pregnancy journey, and ask that you might grow in faith and love at this pivotal moment in your lives.

You may also wish to consecrate your baby to God. If you find it helpful, place your hands on your stomach as a symbol that you are placing your baby in God's hands and trusting the Creator to guide your steps. Surrender both your joys and fears to God as you begin the awesome pilgrimage of pregnancy and parenthood.

You could close with a simple prayer such as this one:

Gracious and loving God, you have blessed us with the gift of new life through this tiny baby, still so fragile and unformed. We know that you have breathed life into this baby and that you already love and care for this precious being. We thank you for the privilege of parenting this baby but realize we cannot do it on our own. Please guide us through the journey of pregnancy. We want to enter this period of preparation in the power of your Holy Spirit. We place ourselves and our baby into your hands, trusting in you for everything that lies ahead through the pregnancy, birth, and the years to come for us as parents. Amen.

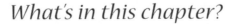

What's in this chapter?

We use stories to understand the events of our lives and to give our lives meaning. But our stories do not simply reflect what has happened to us. They create the realities in which we live: we become the stories that we tell. Reflecting on the stories of our lives can help us to acknowledge where we have come from and what we have experienced, to discover new or forgotten things about ourselves, and to let go of destructive stories. This allows us to live more authentically and abundantly. As we reflect on our stories, we also begin to recognize God's love at work in and through us.

- The power of stories
- How do our stories influence our lives?
- What is the value of reflecting on our stories?
- My story, God's story
- Remembering our stories
- Listening to our stories
- Living forward
- Invitation to Prayer: Write your own story of faith

2

LISTENING TO OUR STORIES

Either you look at the universe as a very poor creation out of which no one can make anything or you look at your own life and your own part in the universe as infinitely rich, full of inexhaustible interest opening out into the infinite further possibilities for study and contemplation and interest and praise. Beyond all and in all is God.

—Thomas Merton, *The Intimate Merton*

Kim . . .

The air was rich with the scent of morning as I stepped out onto the stone path. The path was still wet with the mist that had enfolded the house through the night, and I proceeded carefully on its uneven surface. I was attending a "Life Revision" course,[1] and the retreat leader had invited us to walk the journey of our lives every morning for the week that we were there.

To do this, I mapped out a route in the sprawling garden with a landmark for the end of every seven-year period in my life. I would set out on my walk, reflecting on my life from birth to age seven. Walking slowly and prayerfully, I would allow memories to come rather than trying to call them up. When I reached my first landmark, I planned to stop and jot down all the memories that had come to me during my walk. Then I would walk on toward the next landmark, now focusing on the years of my life between ages seven and fourteen, and so on.

Although I covered the same ground each day, literally and in memory, what I experienced on my walks never failed to surprise me. I felt joy as I remembered precious moments when I knew that I was loved or when I received the affirmation and support of others. And I was deeply moved to remember encounters with God, which often seemed to have occurred when I had reached the end of my own resources. I recognized how these encounters had shifted my perspective, challenged my values and priorities, and invited me to love and be loved more deeply.

There were also painful memories, and tears often fell freely. As I walked the most recent years of my life, I sometimes felt that the wounds left by anorexia were too raw to be touched, particularly those that left me with empty arms, aching to hold a child.

At the end of the week, all of us participating in the course compiled our patchwork memories into a story. We then shared our stories with the other participants. Somehow the process opened up possibilities for new stories to be written into our lives—stories of hope and redemption; stories of "I'm sorry" and "I forgive you"; stories of letting go and of saying hello again[2] in a new way. In a sense, I felt like I was taking up authorship of my own life for the first time, with God as my coauthor.

The course allowed me to reflect on my life, to make peace with my wounds and disappointments, and to begin a journey of restoration and healing. I also learned what it could mean to live my faith consciously and deeply on a daily basis. I was invited to consider my ordinary, everyday life as holy ground, a place of encounter with God rather than an inconvenience that got in the way of my spiritual journey.

The Life Revision course was divided into three blocks, spread out over a year. During the first block, when we walked our life stories, my husband, Dave, and I were coming to terms with the possibility that we would never have our own children and were talking seriously about adoption. By the second block, four months later, I was ecstatically pregnant and beginning to feel the effects of morning sickness. So, for me, the journey of Life Revision also became the journey of my pregnancy.

My pregnancy became an opportunity to experience both my life and God in a new way and to make choices about how I would like my story of motherhood to unfold. This time of conscious reflection and decision making proved to be an incredibly valuable preparation for parenthood.

This book invites you to undertake a similar journey. Every woman enters pregnancy against a complex background of relationships and experiences, events, dreams, beliefs, hopes, and values—the stories of her life. These stories have the power to shape how we manage both our pregnancies and the task of mothering.

Pregnancy seems to offer a natural stopping point, an invitation to look back at where we have come from and where we are right now. So while it may seem strange to begin a book on pregnancy by looking at our past rather than our future, in doing so we are taking a first and very powerful step on our journey of transition into motherhood.

Reflection

- How do you respond to the idea of remembering and reflecting on your life story?
- What would encourage you to do such remembering? What might discourage you?

The Power of Stories

> The universe is made of stories,
>   not of atoms.
>
> —Muriel Rukeyser, poet[3]

Human beings seem to be unique among all living creatures in that we need to make sense of the world around us and our experiences in that world. We are constantly finding ways to interpret, explain, and give meaning to the events of our daily lives. One of our most powerful meaning-making tools is storytelling.

Storytelling has been a feature of all cultures through all ages. Through stories, every gathering or grouping of people has connected, established its identity, been entertained and taught; and through stories people have passed on their legacy of memories, values, traditions, and beliefs from generation to generation.

In some cultures, stories have played a crucial role in people's survival. In the aftermath of the horrifying tsunami that struck on December 26, 2004, the news emerged that certain ancient tribes living in isolation on the islands off India had not suffered a single casualty. Anthropologists concluded that their tradition of storytelling had saved them. Stories about earthquakes and tsunamis were woven into their belief system and the mythology that had passed on from generation to generation. When the earthquake struck, they immediately and unquestioningly moved deeper into the forests, seeking higher ground, and the entire tribe was saved.[4]

Much of the Old Testament and the first few books of the New Testament chronicle the story of God's ongoing involvement in the lives of God's people. Even today, as these stories are told and retold, and new stories are added, people's faith is strengthened and their commitment renewed.

Stories are no less powerful in Western culture, but the stories that transmit our cultural values and beliefs now come to us through television, movies, and the media. If you listen carefully to the conversations of your daily life, you will notice that you spend a great deal of time sharing stories: what's been happening to whom, when, where, why, and how.

Our fascination with stories begins early in childhood, when the stories we hear help us to understand and cope with the world we live in and to find our own place in it. Stories provide a framework on which we can hang our experiences. In fact, research indicates that the brain naturally organizes, retains, and accesses information in story form. This certainly seems to be true of how we come to understand our own lives.

From the time we can speak, we begin to tell stories about our own lives. We talk about what we see, hear, smell, taste, and feel. We talk about the things that happen to us. Gradually, we gather together a series of events that are somehow significant to us and link them together in a sequence over time. This forms the plot of our life story. We tell and retell the story to ourselves and others, and the story grows and gets shaped in these conversations. And the way we talk about our lives profoundly influences the way we live our lives.

Reflection

- What role did stories play in your family when you were growing up?
- What role do they play in your life now?

How Do Our Stories Influence Our Lives?

> The private stories that people have about their lives . . . provide the frame through which people interpret their experiences of life.
>
> —Michael White, *Re-Authoring Lives*[5]

Lindi is seven months pregnant with her first baby. Until now, her pregnancy has been easy, but she is beginning to feel uncomfortable.

She feels as though her stomach has doubled in size in the last two weeks, and she wonders if it will ever stop growing.

She is lying in bed reading when her husband, Zak, comes into the room. "I can certainly see you're pregnant now," he says. "Soon you'll be able to rest your cup of tea on there." Lindi laughs with him, remembering the times early in her pregnancy when she couldn't wait for her bump to start growing and kept asking Zak if she was showing yet. But even while she laughs, she realizes that his words have hurt her, and they set her mind ticking. Zak may just be teasing her gently, but is there more to it?

She remembers that when they went to some friends' house for lunch, Zak discouraged her from taking her swimsuit, saying that he was sure no one would swim. She was furious when everyone except her ended up in the pool on that perfect summer afternoon. Zak also has been quite distant lately and has reached out to touch her less often. Then she recalls how he stared at a young waitress in a restaurant recently. He said he was sure she was the sister of an old school friend, but she did have a stunning figure.

Lindi is gathering a series of apparently unrelated events and linking them together in a story line that goes something like this: Zak finds her new shape unattractive and embarrassing. The story forms in her head as she constructs a whole new meaning for Zak's possibly insensitive but entirely innocent comment. This new reality is so powerful that it leaves her feeling afraid and angry.

Zak climbs into bed beside her and reaches out to pat her tummy. "I had no idea that skin could stretch this much," he says, and Lindi turns on him in a fury. "Why don't you just say that I look fat and ugly and be done with it!" she yells. Her outrage completely bewilders Zak. Tired after a difficult day at work, he just wants a few moments of pleasant conversation with his wife before they turn out the light.

This is not a true story, and perhaps it is a little exaggerated, but many of us can relate to the pattern of thinking that gave rise to Lindi's fury. Lindi wasn't angry because Zak made a comment about her tummy. She was angry because she had constructed a story line that gave new meaning to his comment, and this new meaning angered her. This process of storytelling and meaning-making happens in our minds and in our conversations through most of our waking hours and continues even in our dreams. Our stories are not simply a passive retelling of the "facts" or a simple reflection of reality—they create new facts and call forth new realities.

We tell our stories in conversation, in relationship, in community. Our stories are powerfully influenced by the way other people respond to them as well as by the stories that others tell about us, the expectations they have of us, and the realities these create.

Each of our lives has many stories—about our abilities, struggles, desires, relationships, work, interests, and beliefs.[6] We also have stories about our families, gender, communities of faith, cultural groups, and countries of origin. The beliefs, ideas, and practices of the groups to which we belong and the broader culture in which we live strongly influence the way we understand our lives and the stories we feel free to tell about ourselves. Over time we draw all our stories together into a narrative that we call "Me"—who I am, the face I present to the world. We become the stories that we tell.

Our stories are not simply a passive retelling of the "facts" or a simple reflection of reality—they create new facts and call forth new realities.

Here's an example from my life: I just returned from running and swimming. I thoroughly enjoyed both activities. Fifteen years ago, I could not have predicted I would do this; in fact, I would have laughed at the thought. Throughout my growing-up years, I had a story about myself as not being sporty or athletic.

This story became my reality. I stopped participating in most physical activity. I was therefore unfit and unable to participate in strenuous activity without feeling as though my lungs would explode.

I might have continued with this limiting story for my whole life if I hadn't met Dave. Dave was a keen hiker, and for some un-fathomable reason (Dave says it must have been love) I agreed to go hiking with him. To prepare for the hike, we started running together. At first running was sheer torture, and I hated every minute of it, convinced that I couldn't do it. But as the weeks passed, I came to enjoy it more and more and then even to look forward to our runs. I enjoyed the way my body felt when I was running, entering into the rhythm of breath and pounding feet. I was exultant: I *could* do it!

This knowledge opened up new possibilities for me. My story about myself stretched and grew to accommodate new possible story lines and richer descriptions of who I am. I found myself considering new questions: What else was I capable of that I had never before thought possible? And how might this influence my life?

Reflection

What stories about yourself get in the way of doing or being something that you might enjoy?

What Is the Value of Reflecting on Our Stories?

> [As we remember the past, it] breathes again, in such a way that the present is injected with new life. Previously hidden signifi-cance bursts into conscious awareness. Suddenly, we see clearly what we could not see before. Locked-up feelings find their freedom and in their appropriate expression bring renewed vitality and aliveness. Our sense of who we are and to whom we belong is nourished and sustained.
>
> —Trevor Hudson, *Signposts to Spirituality* [7]

As we each live our stories, certain story lines grow and strengthen in the telling and retelling, while others may be ignored, fade away, and eventually disappear. The exciting possibility, as we reflect on our life stories, is that we can gather together new story lines from the events of our lives that we may never have paid attention to before. We can also let go of stories that are limiting or harmful.

Think about the stories you are telling yourself and others about your pregnancy. Do you talk about pregnancy as a blessing or a curse or something in between? Are there any aspects of your pregnancy that you don't talk about? If you chose one event of your pregnancy thus far and told your story about that event in a new way, perhaps as answered prayer or as an unexpected blessing, what effect might a different perspective have on making meaning of your pregnancy? And what effect could it have on how you experience the months of pregnancy that still lie ahead?

Not only do our stories create the reality in which we act now; they also strongly influence the choices we make about the future.

Not only do our stories create the reality in which we act now, but they also strongly influence the choices we make about the future. During pregnancy we make many choices, and the stories of our lives will shape our decisions. If we take the time to get to know our stories better, we may be better equipped with awareness and insight to make decisions that will work for rather than against us.

Reflecting on our life stories is also a powerful antidote to our natural tendency to look outward for guidance and direction. As we face the prospect of motherhood, we speak to other parents, read books, listen to talk shows, and attend courses. All of these resources are helpful and valuable, but the danger is that we may end up either imitating other people's parenting styles or striving to do the complete opposite of what we have seen others do. As a result, our approach to parenting may be shaped by other people's values and ideals rather than our own, and we may find ourselves trying to live up to an arbitrary set of standards that say we "should" be a certain type of mother.

When we live by sheer effort of will to be all that we "should" be, we ultimately harm ourselves and those around us. Living authentically and abundantly in any role is not about trying harder or achieving more. Instead, it is about becoming ourselves.

Parker J. Palmer encourages us, during times of change and decision making, to pay attention to the old Quaker saying: "Let your life speak." He suggests:

> Before you tell your life what truth and values you have decided to live up to, let your life tell you what truths you embody, what values you represent.[8]

When we take time to reflect on our own lives, we can often begin to discern what we are passionate about, what we stand for, what we value and hold precious. We are able to connect with our desires and purposes and can begin to tell stories about what kinds of mothers we would *prefer* to be rather than being limited by stories about the kinds of mothers we feel we *should* be.

This was Corine's experience during her first pregnancy:

> The thought of becoming a mother started a positive journey within me. I started calling myself a mother as soon as I was pregnant with my first child—I felt that the relationship and the responsibility had started, so I deserved the title!
>
> While I was pregnant, a wonderful and gentle process of self-discovery intensified and added value to "me." I felt that a child would not be mine to mold and dictate to; I could only really work on myself (become more aware of what makes me, me!) and try to be a decent role model for my child.

As Corine discovered more about herself, she realized that her choices regarding pregnancy care and birth options were somewhat outside of the mainstream:

I chose a few "different" routes for pregnancy and birth, and I encountered a lot of opposition to these choices and strong feelings out there about the rightness of the "normal" route . . . but since I was no longer choosing just for myself, I suddenly felt more courageous (and adventurous) about going against the norm, and I definitely became stronger as an individual. It was empowering for me to have to advocate for one who was basically at my mercy and had no voice. The one with no voice helped me to find my own voice!

As we become aware of the stories that shape our lives and underlie our actions and decisions, it becomes possible to interpret and give significance to events in a new way and to tell new stories. We also discover that we don't know all there is to know about ourselves. We are able to see beyond the roles we play and the images we take on and catch a glimpse of our own God-given desires. We discover that our ordinary lives are rich with mystery and possibility.

As we reflect on our stories, we also discover, with Parker J. Palmer, that:

> My life is not only about my strengths and virtues; it is also about my liabilities and my limits, my trespasses and my shadow. An inevitable though often ignored dimension of the quest for "wholeness" is that we must embrace what we dislike or find shameful about ourselves as well as what we are confident and proud of. [9]

So, our stories invite us to face ourselves honestly and accept ourselves as we are. We can then bring all of ourselves into the light of God's love and acceptance. This opens up the possibility of making peace with God, ourselves, and others.

Often, reflecting on our stories leads to a clearing out of the inner junk and clutter that have accumulated over years. Someone once defined forgiveness as "giving up all hope of having had a different past." [10] It seems that that particular hope often keeps alive our resentments, disappointments, and regrets. Perhaps now is the time to let go of our hope for a different past and make space within ourselves for the possibility of a different future. We might find that this gives us more space to share with others.

Your baby will need such space in your life. Babies require our focused attention, and we may be called to draw on greater levels of patience and selfless love than ever before. This becomes very difficult when we are caught up in our own inner turmoil.

As we journey in memory with God and ask God to open our eyes to where we have been blind, we often begin to notice, remember, and rediscover some of the hidden treasure of our lives—those stories about ourselves that were never acknowledged or affirmed or perhaps have never been told. We might also recognize stories about ourselves that are harmful and damaging and that continually get in the way of our relationships with others. Perhaps we can then begin to tell stories that we prefer, that are more in line with our purposes and dreams for our lives and for our babies' lives.

But maybe the most important treasure that our life stories offer is the opportunity to encounter the living God at work in the ordinariness of our lives.

Reflection

What is the most important reason to reflect on your life story?

My Story, God's Story

Your story is God's story, lived out in you, and it is also our story, the story of the whole human family, which cannot be complete until your part of it is told and welcomed.

—Margaret Silf, *Taste and See* [11]

What does Margaret Silf mean by "Your story is God's story"? Perhaps she is thinking about Psalm 139, which celebrates the psalmist's awareness of God's presence with us from our very first moments when God "created [our] inmost being[s]" and "knit [us] together in [our] mother[s']womb[s]" (v. 13, NIV). Or perhaps she is referring to the book of Acts, which tells us that God constantly makes God's self known to us so that we will reach out for God and find that God is not far away at all, for in God "we live and move and have our being" (Acts 17:27-28, NIV).

These scriptures say that God is intimately involved in our lives from beginning to end. From this perspective, to reflect on the story of our lives is to reflect on how God's story is being lived in and through our lives, moment by moment and day by day. Frederick Buechner takes this idea a step further when he suggests:

> Maybe nothing is more important than that we keep track, you and I, of these stories of who we are and where we have come from and the people we have met along the way because it is precisely through these stories in all their particularity . . . that God makes [God's] self known to each of us most powerfully and personally.[12]

I am often tempted to dismiss the value of the story of my day-to-day life. It seems too mundane to have any spiritual value. But because God is present in every moment of my life, my everyday life of mothering, writing, being a wife, eating, running, resting, and washing dishes becomes the very ground in which the seed of God grows. God planted the seed there. God nurtures and tends the seed and keeps calling me back to its care. As I pay attention to the ordinary details of my life, I encounter God at work. Thus, reflecting on my story daily becomes an opportunity to bring together life and prayer, my inner journey and my outward journey.

Our memories can also be a powerful means of grace as we allow God to speak to us and meet us in the midst of them. As we remember, we can begin to identify those moments, events, people, and experiences in which God reached out to us, comforting, guiding, and protecting us. We can also look at our own responses to God's searching love. And we can recognize the inner shifts, storms, and quiet moments in which God spoke and we were changed. This can give us the courage we need to face the challenges of the future.

Reflection

In what ordinary moments of your pregnancy have you especially sensed God's presence with you?

Remembering Our Stories

> Re-membering means, literally, piecing together again what has become fragmented or broken. Ask God for the grace to re-member the fragments of your life in a way that will reveal to you the patterns that are leading towards your wholeness in [God].
> —Margaret Silf, *Landmarks* [13]

Remembering lies at the heart of our faith tradition. On many occasions in scripture, the Israelites are urged to remember how God has led, guided, protected, and loved them. As followers of Christ, remembrance forms the foundation of every communion service and seems fundamental to our stories of growth and spiritual formation.

Various tools can help us with the task of remembering. One is to walk the milestones of your life, as I did during Life Revision. Another tool is a time line of your life, perhaps divided into five- or seven-year stages. On the time line, record all the significant events in your life—occasions like starting school, changing schools, particularly good or bad years at school, deaths and births in your family and among close friends, significant world events and your responses to them, leaving school, studies, first job, relationships (good and bad), getting married, and moving.

Others have found it helpful to make a memory box. A memory box can be any size or shape, as long as it is big enough to store items of significance to you, those mementos that tell or reflect part of the story of who you are. You may include photographs, medals, and certificates; letters you have received and written; special items of clothing; and even favorite toys. You might attach a note to each item, explaining its significance. You could also write or draw an account of the different periods of your life and include this in your box. You can decorate the box in a way that enriches your story and reveals more about you and your life thus far.

A memory box can be a living legacy of who you are when you are expecting your baby and the course your life has taken up until this point. As your child grows, she will love investigating the items in the box with you and hearing your stories.

Another tool for remembering is to use an image such as a river, a road map, or a walking path that winds through various landscapes to represent your life story. For example, you could think of your life as a hike. Where did your hike start out? How would you describe the landscape of your life during your first few years? Was it a level path through cool, green forests, or was it an uphill climb over jagged rocks with the sun beating down on your neck? What periods of your life have traveled through fertile fields, and which have taken you through barren deserts? Where have the places of rest and refreshment been, and what forms have these taken? We can discover much richness just by looking at our lives through the lens of an image like this.

We can also benefit from inviting others to join us in remembering. Leigh found that when she spoke to her sisters about childhood experiences that had been significant for her, they told very different stories. At times it seemed impossible that they could be talking about the same events. But in the end their stories served to challenge and enrich Leigh's own stories about her childhood.

So, as you remember, you may want to choose a few people who have known you through your growing-up years, people who treat you with respect and care, and ask them to share their memories with you. You might ask these people to write you a letter describing their memories of you and your shared experiences.

Reflection

- How would you like to go about remembering your life story?
- Set aside specific times, perhaps spread out over a week or more, to focus on remembering.
- Create a record of your memories in words or pictures.

Listening to Our Stories

> Listening to myself is about listening to a story in the making—a story involving all the different parts of me and my life. It concerns the things that happen to me—outer events and activities—together with my inner perceptions—my thinking, beliefs and attitudes, my feelings, my relationships, my satisfactions and my needs, my past as well as my present.
>
> —Anne Long, *Listening*[14]

Once we have begun remembering the stories of our lives, we can also listen to what those stories are telling us. Such reflective listening is rooted in prayer and constantly draws us back to prayer. As we reflect, we listen for the whisper of God echoing through our memories, and we respond.

We can listen to the stories of our own lives as we would listen to a close friend: with interest and curiosity, with care and attention, and without judgment. Approaching our stories with an attitude of curiosity rather than fear or familiarity opens up the possibility of making new connections and discovering new things about ourselves.

As we exercise our curiosity, we naturally begin to ask questions about our stories. We might ask how one event became linked to another or what effect a particular event had on us. We can listen for themes or threads that seem to run through our lives, and we can also listen for what is not said—the story lines that have been silenced. And we can constantly wonder if there might be a different way to understand our experiences.

As we look back over our lives (or even over the past week or past day), we could ask questions like these:

- What have I received? What have I given?
- What changes have I experienced as positive? as negative?
- What has drawn me away from God, and what has drawn me toward God?
- What in my life has been energizing and life-giving? What has been exhausting and life-draining?
- Which decisions have taken me forward? Which have gotten me stuck? Which have taken me off in new directions?

Clearly, we wouldn't look at all these questions on the same day. Any single question can give us enough to reflect on for days, if not weeks. This process does not need to be rushed, nor is it ever really complete. It is simply an ongoing means to live our lives with greater awareness. In so doing, we become aware of the "underlying movements in our hearts that reveal to us where God is for us and how [God] is forming us."[15]

Reflection

As you look back over the weeks or months that have passed since you discovered you were pregnant, what are you most grateful for? What are you least grateful for?

Living Forward

> It is quite true what Philosophy says: that Life must be under-
> stood backwards. But that makes one forget the other saying: that
> it must be lived—forwards.
> —Søren Kierkegaard, *The Diary of Søren Kierkegaard* [16]

We do not reflect on our life stories in order to get stuck in the past.
We reflect on our stories so we can understand our past and its effect
on us. This allows us to release what needs to be released, to embrace
what needs to be embraced, and to journey on with awareness and
integrity. We do not have to carry our stories with us forever as a
heavy burden. Instead, they can become a source of energy, hope,
caution, and inspiration.

Paying attention to our stories helps us live with integrity, true
to all that we know of ourselves. It also allows us to make new choices
as we "live forwards" with the sacred task of authoring our own
stories and nurturing our children as they begin to author theirs.

Reflection

What will "living forwards" mean for you as you journey
through this pregnancy?

Invitation to Prayer

Scripture is full of stories. Stories are the lifeblood of scripture
because they reveal God's character.

The stories of the people in scripture give us hope, encourage
our faith, guide our decision making, provide comfort, and challenge us. But most of all we see that in the midst of their failures,
doubts, triumphs, and insights God remains true, steadfast, loving,
and powerful enough to change lives. In other words, these persons'
life stories become a testimony to the nature of God.

In your time of prayer, begin to look at the story of your life as a testimony. As you reflect on your life, what significant moments do you recall when you felt particularly aware of God's presence? When did you feel distant from God? Where do you think God was in those moments?

When have you utterly trusted God? At what particular times have you known God loved you? What difference has God made in your life? If someone asked you to explain why you believe God is real, what story could you tell? What key lessons have you learned about yourself, God, and life as you have been led and taught by God's Spirit? Where does your pregnancy fit into your life story?

As you respond to these questions, consider writing a testimony of God's involvement in your life. Write your gospel story—the good news of what God has done and meant in your life. Include incidents in which your faith grew despite difficulties and doubts. Be honest and real—this is *your* story.

Once you have written your faith story, take some time to read over it. Be aware of your thoughts and feelings as you read. What new awareness do you have of God's presence in your life? What do you feel about your own faith?

Now, as with all good news, your story of faith is a gift that is meant to be shared. Think about how you would like to share your faith story and with whom. Perhaps you would simply like to talk it through with your husband or a close friend. Or maybe you would like to copy your written version for your pastor or mentor.

If you share your story with another person, reflect on the experience. How did the person react? What impact do you think it made on him or her to hear about God's work in your life? Spend some time in prayer, thanking God for all that God has done in your life. Ask God to continue to strengthen your faith day by day.

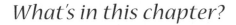

What's in this chapter?

*P*regnancy is a time of transition into a new role. To be able to embrace what lies ahead, we first need to acknowledge what we are letting go of in our pre-pregnancy lives. In this chapter we look at some changes that occur during pregnancy, many of which are beyond our control, and begin to make peace with releasing the way things were.

- Releasing and receiving
- Releasing the way things were in our dreams and expectations
- Releasing the way we were physically
- Releasing the way we were emotionally
- Releasing the way we viewed ourselves
- Mary's example
- Invitation to Prayer: Meditation on a passage of scripture

3

RELEASING THE WAY THINGS WERE

There is no other normative experience in our lives, apart
from our own birth and death, that puts us through such
massive change and transformation in such a relatively brief
amount of time [as pregnancy and childbirth].

—Harriet Lerner, *The Mother Dance*

Leigh . . .

The oldest of five children, I knew the minute my mom was
pregnant without her ever telling me, because she immediately
quit drinking coffee. I did the same as soon as I found out I was
pregnant. I also had nausea, not in the mornings but around the
time I needed to start preparing supper. At times nausea was
convenient because it got me out of cooking, but at other times it
frustrated me.

Being sick wasn't pleasant, but I considered it par for the course.
I expected sickness; in fact, I probably would have been disappointed if I hadn't felt slightly ill and nauseous, because sickness was
a sign of my changed condition. It was almost a rite of passage: I
couldn't really be pregnant if I didn't feel sick.

Then there was the tiredness. It wasn't the kind of tiredness I'd experienced before, which had included the exhaustion of long-distance travel and many days of sightseeing on foot, or the weariness of long hours studying, or the tiredness of a good, hard day's work. This tiredness was a heavy weight that I couldn't shake off and had to drag around with me.

All these symptoms indicated that because of pregnancy my life had changed. But there were also many ways in which my life had not changed, particularly in the early stages of pregnancy. I looked the same, perhaps a little paler than usual, but there were no outward signs that I was pregnant. I continued in my job. My husband continued in his job. My doctor visits were spread out. Everyone asked a few polite questions about when the baby was due, but childbirth was still such a long way off that it didn't merit more than a couple of sentences of conversation. It was too early to prepare rooms, go shopping, or do anything that would tell me and the world that I was facing a monumental change in my life that was both incredibly exciting and extremely daunting.

Each pregnancy is a watershed in women's lives.

I knew, though, that I had changed and would continue to change. My body, mind, emotions, relationships, and even my dreams for the future were caught up in this new experience, and I could not control or stop the changes. I was beginning to let go of what my life had been like before I became pregnant, even though my daily life remained largely unaffected.

Each pregnancy is a watershed in women's lives. Perhaps the first awareness we have that our life is about to change dramatically happens the moment we discover we are pregnant. On finding out I was pregnant, I was overwhelmed by a flood of emotions—delight, fear, wonder, terror, and doubt. I knew that I had stepped into an unknown world that would change my life forever. I could never go back to the way things were before I became pregnant.

This awareness often returns with an equal intensity when we feel our baby's movements within us for the first time. When you sense those first flutterings of life, the reality that you are pregnant and are going to be a parent becomes even more pressing. The gentle knocking is a reminder that inside you waits a little being who will be part of your life story forever.

And the ripples of change do not end with us. We are changed by our children, they are changed by us, and they grow up to change the world. God's world is enriched by each new and unique person who lives out his or her story. Each one's life, however brief or long, makes a difference to the stories of those around him or her.

All change involves leaving behind something known in order to move toward the new and unknown. It means releasing the way things were in order to embrace the way things are and the way things will be. As Kim said, understanding our past is important, but our lives are meant to be lived in the present and into the future.

This chapter looks at our responses to some of the changes we experience during our pregnancy. We will also explore some things we may need to let go of and how to do that. Finally, we spend some time reflecting on how Mary managed the changes relating to her pregnancy with Jesus.

Reflection

What have you had to let go of since finding out you were pregnant?

Releasing and Receiving

> God, grant me the serenity
> to accept the things I cannot change,
> courage to change the things I can,
> and the wisdom to know the difference.
>
> —Attributed to Reinhold Niebuhr

Some changes in life happen whether we choose them or not, like aging or the way our bodies respond to pregnancy. However, we can decide to make certain changes; for example, we can always choose to change our attitude. Acknowledging those changes we cannot control, being honest about our feelings, and learning to accept the changes with grace can empower us. When we deliberately release those things we can do nothing about, we make ourselves more available to receive the blessings that the new brings. Choosing to release the way things were before we conceived permits us to more fully embrace all that pregnancy can teach us.

Releasing the way things were involves saying good-bye to certain aspects of our pre-pregnancy lives, such as the freedom to choose

Choosing to release the way things were before we conceived permits us to more fully embrace all that pregnancy can teach us.

how we spend our time, our pre-parenting relationship with our husband, perhaps our career plans, and what occupies our mind. We can let go joyfully with anticipation or reluctantly with pain and regret; usually we feel a mixture of both. As we open our hands to let go of the old, we free ourselves to accept what lies ahead and to receive the gifts that await us during our pregnancy.

The process of releasing and receiving is also an integral part of our spiritual journey. We let go of pride in order to receive other people's loving generosity. We let go of preconceived notions in order to gain new insights. We let go of painful memories in order to begin afresh. As we begin to let go of such things, we're not doing it alone. God, who understands the nature of change, invites and empowers us on the journey of change.

Ultimately, this spiritual process is about gradually releasing more and more of ourselves to God. We place all that we are: our hopes, dreams, and fears; our past, present, and future—our whole lives—into the hands of God. Then we experience true freedom, because we are no longer weighed down but instead open to all that life offers, especially now, through this new life forming within us.

Reflection
What would you like to release into God's hands now?

Releasing the Way Things Were in Our Dreams and Expectations

> Pregnancy is an event largely beyond our control, and there is no one right or wrong way to move through the experience.
> —Harriet Lerner, *The Mother Dance*[1]

As a young girl, did you ever daydream with your friends about how many children you would have, how many boys and girls, and even imagine what you would name them? There was always someone who wanted twins! Your own experience of siblings certainly played a big role in your ideas. I was dead set on having boys after growing up in a household of all girls. Many of us grew up with preconceived ideas as to what constituted the perfect combination of children to make a happy family. However, reality seldom matches our ideals.

For instance, finding out we are having more than one baby can be a huge shock. It was for Caroline, who definitely did not want two babies at once. Fortunately, she found out fairly early in her pregnancy that she was carrying twins, so she had time to adjust to the idea. Janet, on the other hand, was delighted to find out she was pregnant with twins. For her it was an answer to a prayer. She and her husband had struggled to conceive, so they believed this might be their only chance to have a family. But at the same time she was grateful they weren't having triplets!

Many people place a great deal of value on the gender of a child. In some cultures a man has not proved himself unless he "produces" a male child. Growing up in a family of four girls, I often heard the seemingly lighthearted teasing my dad received from his friends and wondered how it affected him. A surprise baby—a boy—was born into our family when I was eighteen. I cannot honestly say that my parents were any more pleased to have a son at last than they had been to have four girls, but perhaps my dad's chest did puff up a little more and my mom's chin lifted a little higher.

But their longing could have been in the other direction as well. My husband grew up in a happy family of two children in which he had an older sister, and for him the perfect arrangement might have been for us to have the same. For some reason I felt pressured that our first child should be a girl. Because we decided not to find out the gender of our baby before it was born, I eventually convinced my husband and myself that we were having a boy so that he would not be disappointed.

Whether we acknowledge them or not, we all have had dreams or expectations regarding pregnancy—even if that expectation was that we would never get pregnant. Perhaps you have a story about yourself as not being the "maternal" type, as being more career or service oriented, but now you are pregnant. Perhaps you became pregnant sooner than you anticipated, or perhaps your pregnancy was unplanned.

Maybe you needed medical intervention in order to get pregnant, and because the conception was not "natural," your dream about how you "should" have become pregnant has been shattered. Perhaps you are expecting twins and cannot imagine what your life will be like coping with more than one baby. Perhaps you always pictured dressing up your precious little girl in pink and showing her off to the world, and now you are having a boy. Or you may feel pressure to continue your husband's family name, and instead of the much-anticipated boy, you are having a girl.

The circumstances of our pregnancy seldom fit how we had carefully designed it in our minds. We may not achieve what we or society believe is the "perfect" pregnancy, with the "perfect" number of children, the "perfect" age gaps between them, and the "perfect" genders. (For further discussion of the so-called "perfect" pregnancy, see the next chapter, "Recognizing Myths.") We may feel that we have not gotten pregnant at the right age, at the right time, with the right person, with the right child. This is when we need the serenity to accept the things we cannot change. And in order to accept what is, we first need to let go of what might have been. Trevor Hudson suggests that moving toward acceptance and serenity can be a gradual process:

> This kind of acceptance seldom comes easily. We need all the grace and help and power that God can give. But when we are able to accept what cannot be changed, the seed of peace planted in our hearts begins to germinate and grow. As time goes by, we gain the precious gift of serenity.[2]

Reflection

- What expectations of your pregnancy have not been fulfilled?
- Make a list of all the blessings you have been given.

Releasing the Way We Were Physically

> Prayer was always meant to be part of our everyday lives, part of our bodies, part of all our actions.
> —Flora Slosson Wuellner, *Prayer and Our Bodies*[3]

Pregnancy triggers a natural process over which we have no control. Our bodies may feel strange and alien: we cannot predict what food we will crave or react against, when we might be hit by leg cramps, or what shape our bodies will take as the baby grows. I must admit I was quite captivated by the idea of having a neat, round ball up front as my pregnant shape, with no pushed-out belly button, of course.

Well, I didn't get the pushed-out belly button, but I was more pregnant around my thighs and buttocks than all neatly in front. During pregnancy, one of the things we need to release is the idea that we can control our bodies.

Nausea is definitely beyond our control and is probably the most telltale sign that we are pregnant. I was fortunate that my nausea was mild and lasted for only three months. Other women are not so lucky. Debby had her head over the toilet bowl for most of her first trimester. Poor Elize felt sick her entire pregnancy and even threw up during labor! In such circumstances we need to hang on to the words "This too shall pass." At least we know that even though it may be a long nine months, it will be only nine months, and at the end we will be rewarded with a precious baby. This knowledge can help us find the strength and courage to persevere.

During pregnancy, one of the things we need to release is the idea that we can control our bodies.

Perhaps the most debilitating aspect of early pregnancy, which we often underestimate, is the tiredness. The overwhelming exhaustion I experienced during my first trimester required me to adjust the pace of my life, because I just could not fit as much into the day as I had before. This meant a slowing down and a stillness that I was not used to, and I rebelled against it at first. I believed my fatigue was all in my mind, and if I just tried hard enough, I would be able to pick up my previous pace and variety of life. It never happened.

I had to change my expectations of what I could do in a day. I began to learn that the slower pace brought its own rewards in drawing closer to God, understanding myself better, and enjoying life's simpler pleasures. I was able to spend more time in prayer, creative hobbies, and appreciating our beautiful world.

In addition to nausea and fatigue, one of the greatest physical adjustments pregnant women have to make relates to changes in their size and weight. Unfortunately, we live in a culture that places a high value on slimness, and many women strive to maintain a shape and level of fitness in keeping with what is "acceptable." As they increase in size and weight during the course of pregnancy, many women feel themselves judged by society's standards and experience a loss of self-esteem. Naomi Wolf certainly did:

> As a heavy woman in society (I hoped temporarily, but who knew?) I felt as if I'd slipped several notches down in the social hierarchy of the world. My self-image had gotten skinned on the fast slide down. [4]

In the movie *Two Weeks Notice*, Hugh Grant's character makes a blunder when he asks a woman he is interviewing when her baby is due, only to discover she is not pregnant! That in-between stage when you are just starting to show can be the most awkward, because people are too embarrassed to ask anything in case they make a similar error. So women at this stage usually have to endure quizzical looks and even blunt stares, which can either make you want to push out your stomach a little more to show off your new roundness or to shrink away in embarrassment at what people might be thinking.

Actually, many women embrace the opportunity pregnancy offers them to not worry about their weight or about what other people think. When Alison, author of *I Have Life*, was asked to identify the worst aspect of her pregnancy, she replied, "The fact that I can't fit into any of my clothes, but on the other hand I don't want to—I'm pregnant!" Janine took a similar approach:

> I had no control over what shape and size my body took, but whatever it did, it was acceptable, and nobody had the right to say otherwise because it was a course of nature. And it was a wonderful feeling to be slightly unconcerned about those few extra pounds.

Fortunately, attitudes are changing toward the shape of pregnant women's bodies and what they represent. When I was pregnant fifteen years ago, mothers-to-be wore flowing, tentlike outfits, supposedly to hide their bulging tummies. Today women wear garments that proudly show off their pregnant shape. It's a great way of announcing to the world, "Hey, look, another human being is under construction!"

In fact, our new awareness of our body can make us feel more sensual and womanly. Many men also find a pregnant woman's curves sexy. So instead of complaining about how our body is changing, we can choose to delight in it.

Pregnancy can also give us a new appreciation of our body's intricate workings. We can marvel at its capacity to support life and its flexibility in coping with all the changes a growing baby brings. The delight we take in our body can become a prayer of thanks and praise to the God who created us as women and declared creation to be good.

Reflection

- What has been your greatest physical adjustment during pregnancy?
- What have you appreciated or enjoyed most about the changes in your body thus far?

Releasing the Way We Were Emotionally

> In your journeying may you find the embrace of acceptance; in your acceptance may you find your song; in your song may you find liberation: the holy coming to birth in you.
> —Jan L. Richardson, *Sacred Journeys*[5]

Perhaps what pregnant women get teased about the most (apart from food cravings) are their dramatic mood swings. At some stage during their pregnancy, many expectant moms burst into floods of tears, apparently for no reason; feel panic-stricken and keep checking and rechecking to make sure that the stove is off; or get angry and resentful if their craving for pickles and chocolate is not met immediately.

It is understandable that with all the hormones raging through your body during pregnancy, you will go through mood swings and intense emotional states. Still, it is embarrassing to suddenly find tears pouring down your face at a board meeting or while standing in the line at a supermarket. However, despite the influence of hormones, these emotions are real and may take us by surprise during pregnancy. One such emotion might be sadness at what we are losing.

During pregnancy most of us lose our figure, albeit temporarily. We may lose our status as professionals or workers, or feel as if we have had to give up our own space. We may feel a loss of independence, because we no longer have just ourselves to consider. Debby described it this way:

> I guess my pregnancy made me realize how responsible I was for the well-being of the baby inside me and what an awesome responsibility being a parent is. I learned to be less self-centered. My baby and its well-being became more important than anything. I didn't just see myself as an individual anymore.

The emotional response to these losses can also easily be dismissed as a pregnant woman's "typical" moodiness. Our sense of sadness seems at odds with our happiness and fulfillment, and we may not be able to pinpoint where it is coming from. So we may deny or simply ignore our darker feelings. The problem with this is that emotions are not easily dismissed and tend to persist until they are paid some attention.

Fear is another common emotion for pregnant women, so common that we have dedicated a whole chapter to it: "Facing Fear." In the chapter "Becoming Whole," we look at other unexpected emotional responses we may experience during pregnancy and how we can manage them.

Experiencing some sense of loss in pregnancy is normal. It indicates the enormous change we are going through. It means that not only our bodies but also our minds and emotions are coming to terms with a new way of being. Going through a period of adjustment and transition can be painful. Almost all significant changes give rise to these feelings, even when the change is desired. When we see our feelings in this context, we can accept them, talk about them, and let them be, in order to move through them to a place of peace.

Reflection

- What has been your greatest emotional challenge during pregnancy?
- To whom can you talk about your feelings?

Releasing the Way We Viewed Ourselves

> When change-winds swirl through our lives, . . . they often call us to undertake a new passage of the spiritual journey: that of confronting the lost and counterfeit places within us and releasing our deeper, innermost self—our true self. They call us to come home to ourselves, to become who we really are.
> —Sue Monk Kidd, *When the Heart Waits* [6]

Linda told us of the following encounter with her friend Penny:

> Penny and I are sitting under the wisteria having iced tea. "You know," she says animatedly, "I never realized how important being pregnant was to me. All my life I struggled with being accepted—I never felt complete as a person. My choices felt so limited. I went to college, got a job, jumped into marriage too quickly, got

divorced, and then married again—all without any particular thought or consideration. Within two months I was pregnant. Instead of feeling panic, I suddenly felt worthy of something."

Linda says Penny seemed agitated yet relieved to share her story, as if someone had finally uncorked the bottle. Penny continued,

It probably sounds silly now, but then it felt like a remarkable thing had happened to me. My husband wasn't ready for the pregnancy, and certainly our marriage wasn't. I was ill equipped to care for a baby, but deep inside I believed that I'd done something that would enable me to feel accepted. I needed so much and believed that my baby would fulfill my needs—the need to be loved, recognized, and acknowledged. My expectations of pregnancy were that I'd finally be fully accepted into society.

In one way or another, pregnancy affects the stories we tell about ourselves—what we usually call our self-image or self-esteem. Who we are, how we judge our worth, and what we mean to others become challenging questions during pregnancy. We may need to use this opportunity to release destructive beliefs or ideas in order to embrace a truly wholesome and life-giving understanding of who we are.

As women, we have many different roles, depending on our various relationships and activities. We may be friend, daughter, wife, colleague, boss, lover, or sister; now we add mother to the list. What does this role mean for you? Does it add to or subtract from your life?

While the women's movement has played a powerful and important role in opening up opportunities for women to choose how they will live their lives, one unfortunate side effect has been the devaluing of the role of motherhood. Women are almost discouraged from desiring motherhood because it has been characterized as a burden or an obstacle to achieving their full potential. However, the women who responded to our questionnaires seem to say that, despite the bad press it has received, motherhood is desirable and profoundly fulfilling for many women.

Linda, who struggled with the concept of motherhood and then with infertility for a number of years, wrote:

> I came to realize that I'd underrated my own capacity for mother-hood—that indeed, being or wanting to be a mother did not mean relinquishing my many other worthy facets. I realized that it would be helpful for me to reassess the basis on which I was assessing my worth as a woman and to take my first steps toward wholeness.

For many women, pregnancy and motherhood provide a sense of fulfillment and meaning unmatched by any other life experience. In embracing the pleasures of motherhood, as well as their own capacity to cope with its challenges, many women emerge from pregnancy with a new perspective on themselves and the meaning of their lives. This is how Corine described it:

> I think I grew up a bit while I was pregnant and started viewing myself more as a relevant and important being. I felt very special and believed that I was the envy and talk of the town. It was lovely to carry a child and do what only a woman can do!

Many other women described the pleasure of being pregnant and its profound impact on how they saw themselves:

> I loved the feeling of these babies growing inside me, and I was proud of it. I would say that in my life, my pregnancies were the two times that I felt most secure and confident about myself, perhaps because I knew that I had a purpose: to nurture my babies. Only I could do it, and I was doing a good job of it. I felt useful and a real sense of worth . . . I felt mature and responsible.
>
> —Janine

> The process of growth was awesome to me. As our baby grew and developed . . . I evolved personally into someone I respected and loved being.
>
> —Cheryl

[During my first pregnancy] I felt like a real woman! . . . I loved my pregnant body; it was a great joy to feel the baby move inside me, and a very special bond developed between me and the baby.

—Sara

However, some women experience a profound sense of losing their own distinct identities during their pregnancies:

I'm sure I gave myself a status, an importance of being someone each time I became pregnant. I suppose I had a sense of achievement—I didn't dwell on any sense of self, but I'm sure I projected myself through my babies—and lost myself along the way.

—Lorraine

During my second pregnancy I felt like a nothing. I was a wife, mother, daughter, sister, friend, but I had lost the sense of me. I became anxious, emotional, and lost self-confidence and self-esteem. Five months after the birth, I was diagnosed with post-partum depression, so it has been a long journey to regain that sense of self. But I am getting there again with the help and grace of God.

—Sara

Fiona became extremely ill during her third pregnancy. She struggled with her feeling that everyone seemed to value the baby's well-being above hers:

When I was so ill, I suffered because I really felt that once the baby was born, I would recover (which I did), but no one wanted to put me first, and I felt like a pregnancy instead of a person in my own right.

Undoubtedly pregnancy significantly shapes our ideas about who we are and how we view our place in the world. Our pregnancy becomes an opportunity to explore new stories about ourselves, not based on our roles or positions or how others see us. It provides a chance to discover the story that God tells about us—which does not depend on anything we do, or how we do it, but on who we are.

God looks at us with love, kindness, and great compassion at all times, whether or not we are pregnant. Zephaniah 3:17 tells us that God takes great delight in us, calms and quiets us with divine love, and rejoices over us with singing. I wonder what song God is singing over me right now? What song is God singing over you? Scripture says that it is a song of rejoicing and delight. I wonder what effect it would have on us if we could hear, just once, the words of God's song for us.

Our sense of identity and self-image need to be rooted in God's love for us rather than in our success or lack of success in any particular role. In his first letter, John almost shouts with joy and celebration, "How great is the love the Father has lavished on us, that we should be called children of God!" (1 John 3:1, NIV). Even as we are in the process of becoming mothers, our first and truest identity is as children of God.

Reflection

In what ways has pregnancy affected your sense of self?

Mary's Example

> Glory to God in the highest,
> and on earth peace to [all people]
> on whom his favor rests.
>
> —Luke 2:14, NIV

There is no denying that pregnancy ushers in change for all women, but for Mary, the mother of Jesus, pregnancy represented nothing less than a radical shift in the direction she had thought her life would take. It is unlikely that giving birth to the Messiah played a major role in her childhood daydreams. She certainly would not have dreamed of or even desired to get pregnant before marriage and at such a young age. She couldn't have wanted to undertake a strenuous journey during the last days of her pregnancy in order to get to Bethlehem for the census. And I don't think that anything could have prepared her for giving birth in a stable. As much as she may have been comforted by the knowledge that the child she carried was from God, could she have grasped what this really meant?

We will have to be content to wonder in regard to many questions about Mary's pregnancy, but we do know that Mary responded to each unexpected challenge with dignity and faith. She believed that her life was serving an important purpose for God, therefore she willingly gave herself to all that would best serve that purpose.

"I am the Lord's servant," Mary answers the angel Gabriel (Luke 1:38, NIV). Then she says, "May it be to me as you have said." Mary makes an active choice to surrender to the will of God. With these words she decides to take on all that her pregnancy may mean for her, consequences both difficult and wonderful. We can learn a great deal from Mary.

Mary's story also guides us in other ways. At the Annunciation the angel's first words to Mary are, "Greetings, you who are highly favored! The Lord is with you" (Luke 1:28, NIV). We can receive these words for ourselves too. We may not be carrying the "Son of the Most High" (v. 32, NIV), but nevertheless we have the awesome privilege of nurturing a child within us, a unique and loved creation of

No matter how positive or negative the circumstances of our pregnancy, we can know in our minds and hearts that we are not alone.

God. We have been favored in bearing this responsibility. We too can claim the promise "The Lord is with you." No matter how positive or negative the circumstances of our pregnancy, we can know in our minds and hearts that we are not alone. God knows us, walks with us, and accompanies us throughout our life journey.

Mary also shows us how to make sense of our lives in the light of our faith in God. Luke tells us she "treasured all these things in her heart" (Luke 2:51, NIV). Treasuring in our heart involves an attitude of observation, awareness, reflection, and thankfulness. The journey of pregnancy offers an opportunity for treasuring and reflecting, for marking and holding dear the many special moments, such as the first sign of life within us, the first ultrasound, even the first time our zipper does not close! Like Mary, we can learn to treasure the bad with the good, the painful with the joyful, and the losses with the gifts. All become a rich resource that can build and grow us, shaping us into strong women who live with maturity, integrity, and love.

Reflection

- What stands out for you as the most difficult change in your pregnancy so far?
- What have you enjoyed most about your pregnancy?

Invitation to Prayer

One of the privileges of being God's children is that God continually reaches out and speaks to us in our everyday lives. One way God communicates is through the Bible. Just as God spoke to Mary, God also can speak into our circumstances through scripture.

During this time of prayer, look more closely at Luke 1:26-38, the passage describing the encounter between Mary and the angel. As you meditate on these verses, use the gift of your imagination and listen for what God is saying to you.

Ask God to guide your time and to speak the words you most need to hear today. Pray that you may know God's presence throughout this time of prayer. Then read Luke 1:26-38 slowly and, if possible, out loud, several times.

The Lord is saying to you, just as the angel Gabriel said to Mary, "Greetings, you who are highly favored! The Lord is with you." How do you respond to this greeting? What does being "highly favored" mean for you? If you decide to accept God's version of the story of your life—that you are "highly favored"—how might that affect the way you live your life today? In what ways do you know that God is with you?

Now allow yourself to share your heart with God. Tell the Lord about everything that's happened to you and within you since learning of your pregnancy. Tell God how you are feeling about all the changes that are happening in your mind and body.

After you've spoken your heart, hear these words: "Do not be afraid, [your name]; you have found favor with God." Despite everything you feel, because of everything you feel, and in the midst of everything you feel, God deeply loves and appreciates you. You have found favor with God. You are "precious and honored" in God's sight (Isa. 43:4, NIV).

Do you feel ready to embrace all that your pregnancy will mean to you? Can you choose to welcome your experience of pregnancy as a means of growth and new life, not only for your unborn baby but also for you? Are you able to accept that God's purpose for you at this moment in time is the present reality of your pregnancy? If you find yourself answering yes to these questions, you may want to echo Mary's words of surrender: "I am the Lord's servant. May it be to me as you have said" (Luke 1:38, NIV).

What's in this chapter?

During pregnancy, we come across various myths—
strange beliefs about pregnancy and birth that
seem true but aren't. Some are quite funny, but others
can be destructive. In this chapter we look at what myths
are and how they arise, and we address some common
myths about pregnancy. Our goal is to develop strategies for recognizing myths and to discern the truth that
brings freedom and joy.

- What is a myth?
- Myth: Pregnancy is either heaven or hell
- Myth: All information has value
- Myth: It's got to be perfect
- The deceptive power of myths
- The liberating power of truth
- Invitation to Prayer: A reflection on Jesus' state-
  ments about himself

4

RECOGNIZING MYTHS

The great enemy of truth is very often not the lie—deliberate, contrived and dishonest—but the myth—persistent, persuasive and unrealistic.

—John F. Kennedy, *Mother of All Myths*

Linda. . .

I am having lunch with a group of women, some who are pregnant (like me) and some who are moms of babies or toddlers. The main topic of conversation is pregnancy, and we're talking about gender:

"Well, my midwife said that when you're nauseous throughout the pregnancy, it means you're having a girl."

"My prenatal instructor says that if you have a high libido and if your hair is thicker or grows quickly, you're carrying a girl."

Connie turns to me and says, "Well, then I'm having a girl—look at the hair on my arms."

We compare arms while someone explains that it's pretty certain you're having a girl if you carry your weight fairly evenly distributed around your body.

I go home and tell Francois: "Well, seeing that I had only three weeks of nausea, would rather have a bowl of broccoli than sex, have thinning hair, and am carrying all my weight up front, we must be having a boy!"

I didn't have a boy—Connie did. And because I didn't want to know the baby's gender beforehand, everyone seemed to feel compelled to share a theory about figuring out our baby's gender. I knew these ideas were hogwash, but sometimes they caught me unaware when I heard them from medical personnel and other respected figures. Of course I knew that the way I carried my unborn child had no scientific bearing on the baby's gender, but when "experts" made comments, and people we trusted referred to our baby as a boy, it started to influence our thinking.

For many of us, everything about pregnancy and childbirth is so new that we may find it difficult to discern truth from myth.

Many ideas you will encounter about pregnancy seem laughable. For example, have you heard that now you should be eating for two? Or that to bring on labor, you need to eat spicy food or make love or drink castor oil? Normally we would dismiss such theories without a second thought, but depending on who is discussing them, you may find yourself wondering if they could be true. For many of us, everything about pregnancy and childbirth is so new that we may find it difficult to discern truth from myth. Myths capitalize on our fears, insecurities, and ignorance. So before we know it, we have picked up a belief, like a bit of fluff that attaches itself to us, and soon we find ourselves living up to it.

This chapter is about myths: those strange beliefs that seem true but do not bring us life and goodness, which are what God intended truth to bring. We will look at what myths are and how they arise. We will also explore a few of the many myths related to pregnancy and think about how to recognize myths.

The kinds of myths that suggest a link between hair growth on our arms and the gender of our baby are more amusing than concerning. They are easy to spot a mile off and unlikely to cause us distress.

More concerning are the myths that have been woven into the fabric of thought in our society and that influence the way we talk and think about pregnancy. The danger, as we saw in "Listening to Our Stories," is that the way we speak about our life experiences—the language and vocabulary we use—actually shapes those experiences. Even myths that seem quite harmless on the surface can have undesirable effects. We therefore need to discern what is myth and what is truth. Only truth can bring us life in fuller measure and the freedom to enjoy our pregnancy.

Reflection
What strange ideas have you encountered so far in your pregnancy?

What Is a Myth?

> [A myth is] nothing more than ancient gossip.
> —Stanislaw, *Webster's New World Dictionary of Quotable Definitions*[1]

A myth is a belief that a person came up with in order to explain his or her experience of a particular event or phenomenon. Myths help us make sense of our lives and the world around us. Passed on through stories, in the media, or in general conversation, they seep into our knowledge until it seems that they have always been there—they simply become "common sense." So myths may appear to be reliable and reasonable by virtue of their widespread acceptance, when they are actually false.

As newly pregnant moms, we are susceptible to accepting the myths around pregnancy as truth. We may feel insecure and a little daunted by pregnancy, so we rely on what others tell us and assume that they're telling the truth. We trust advice and believe what we see, hear, and read. We may feel that we don't know enough to challenge what the experts say or what is considered common knowledge.

What are some of these myths surrounding pregnancy and motherhood? One is that motherhood is instinctive—because I'm a woman, I should automatically know what to do when I'm pregnant and giving birth. Another myth is that having children is a woman's purpose and destiny and that all women want to have children. The flip side of this coin is the belief that women who have not had children, through choice or circumstance, are incomplete somehow.

A popular myth that we encounter in every advertisement featuring a mother-to-be is that pregnancy is a glowing experience. Because pregnancy is regarded as such a blessing (myth or truth?), we often assume that we should look and feel radiant. If this is true, then we should also never feel frustrated, overwhelmed, or resentful. If your pregnancy was pure bliss from beginning to end, please let us know, because we have not yet come across a woman who never had one negative thought, one painful emotion, or one bad hair day during her pregnancy!

In the three sections that follow, we examine a few powerful myths of pregnancy a little more closely. We will work toward developing strategies for discerning truth from myth so that we can let go of unhelpful beliefs.

Myth: Pregnancy Is Either Heaven or Hell

> I would think to myself: I am a bad woman because I am not continually blissful at the imminence of the being in my belly. I am a bad woman because I am not perpetually floating on air, radiant as someone in a shampoo ad, beaming.
>
> —Naomi Wolf, *Misconceptions*[2]

Is pregnancy anything like you imagined? There are two popular and completely contradictory myths about pregnancy in circulation, and you may have picked up one or the other or a mixture of the two. According to these myths, pregnancy is either heaven or hell. The "pregnancy as heaven" myth suggests that pregnancy is a radiant, contented time filled with tranquillity and serenity. This is the pregnancy magazine image of a glowing woman with enough newfound energy to paint the entire house and a sunny disposition that oozes calm and well-being.

The "pregnancy as hell" myth paints a completely different picture: an image of utter wretchedness, often portrayed in movies featuring a pregnant woman. This myth focuses on the nausea, ballooning size, and depression that must be endured until a climactic birth. Labor usually begins with one's water breaking during the most solemn moment of a wedding or in a crowded supermarket, and the birth is depicted in various undignified, improbable images: huge women huffing on the car's backseat or pushing and screaming in the midst of a national crisis or disaster.

Our expectations of pregnancy may be optimistic and idealistic or fearful and cynical, depending on which myth attached itself to us most firmly.

So, our expectations of pregnancy may be optimistic and idealistic or fearful and cynical, depending on which myth attached itself to us most firmly. Either way, these expectations will continue to be shaped by the media and by stories we hear from other women. Even the accounts of our own birth can influence our perception of pregnancy. Unfortunately, the media deals in stereotypes, and we can seldom generalize from other people's stories.

When women are open and honest about their feelings and expectations without imposing them on others, they can explore what pregnancy is really like. Kim shared this:

Most people expected me to be thrilled and excited all the time. The joy was there—it never left me—but it by no means summed up the totality of my experience. I was also absolutely exhausted—

and frustrated because I was so exhausted. I was nauseous and achy and tearful and fragile—and ashamed of my own fragility.

Lisa and Lauren echoed these thoughts:

I wish I had known that not everybody glows and radiates, and that this is quite normal. That not everyone is filled with this amazing "mother's love". . . and that pregnancy is also uncomfortable, burdensome, and restricting sometimes.

—Lisa

I hated being pregnant both times, even though I had good pregnancies. I hated the cumbersomeness, the tiredness, and all the little things that go with it. When I told people about this, they were shocked.

—Lauren

The truth is, pregnancy is neither heaven or hell—it's a bit of both! At times we glow. We also have times of frustration and discomfort. The proportion you have of each will depend on the unique nature of your pregnancy.

No one can tell you what it will be like for you, only what it was like for her. Pregnancy may bring many commonalities, but we must remember that each pregnancy is different. The fact that being pregnant is a common occurrence doesn't mean that we don't experience it individually: God treasures our uniqueness. Let's celebrate our diversity.

Reflection

- In what way has your pregnancy felt different from the "norm"?
- Which myth about pregnancy—heaven or hell—is closer to your story about your own pregnancy?

Myth: All Information Has Value

> Pity the pregnant woman! No sooner are the congratulations over than she finds she is subject to an endless stream of information, advice and warnings. Her every action will be observed and monitored, her every deviation noted. . . . every aspect of a pregnant woman's behaviour is open to scrutiny, risk assessment and control.
>
> —Aminatta Forna, *The Mother of All Myths* [3]

When I got pregnant, I became preoccupied with the baby and with reading about her development, my diet, and all the lists of dos and don'ts. I eagerly pursued information and needed to know about things that had never touched my life before.

So much about pregnancy is unknown to us. We cannot truly know how we will feel, how our bodies will respond, how our babies will develop, or how people will react. In this hazy atmosphere, we often have more questions than answers and seek out information to decrease our anxiety. Unfortunately, our longing to know makes us vulnerable to the ever-ready and often conflicting "guidance" that is available.

I certainly had not anticipated having armchair experts, the media, and a variety of interested people from my obstetrician to my hairdresser all vying for my attention! First there were the pregnancy magazines (I couldn't resist them when I went to the supermarket), television programs, newspaper articles, and Web sites. They appeared to speak with scientific authority and had the status of being in print, so their statements had the power to persuade and convince me. But this meant that at times I was captivated and misled by powerful words and images.

I also found that people assumed I would want to know their tales. They launched into birthing accounts, pregnancy problems, and "expert" advice. Everybody had the most trustworthy pregnancy manual, the latest trend, the best obstetrician, and the most informative magazine.

An enormous amount of information and advice is available, but its sheer scale can intimidate. Half of the things I read and heard seemed to contradict the other half, and I often found it difficult to discern the truth. With so much information to wade through, we can't always be certain whether we're being hindered or helped.

That was certainly the experience of these women:

Shortly after the news of my pregnancy broke, I took refuge in the written word as I was inundated with advice, which alternatively contradicted and agreed with each other. I had never realized the world contained such a wellspring of experts on matters such as pregnancy, birth, and breast-feeding. As my husband is often fond of saying, "Good advice is something that should be passed on because you're certainly not going to use it yourself!"

—Fiona

The magazines had suggestions about what I should be doing, thinking, buying, and I would find my attempts at doing this pregnancy thing "right" lacking in comparison. . . . More compelling, however, were the images of expectant mothers on almost every page—all well-groomed, glowing, serene, busily preparing for their new arrival, smiling at the camera, or gazing thoughtfully into the distance. Their collective impact was powerful. And it was an image that was completely foreign to most of my pregnancy experience.

—Kim

I wish I'd known to stay away from everyone who'd had a baby so that I wouldn't have to listen to all the war stories, including the gory details. I very much appreciated constructive advice, but often there was just too much information!

—Cheryl

So what do we do? Should we take Cheryl's advice and stay away from everyone who's ever had a baby? Should we avoid magazine articles and news programs? The problem is, we do need help and advice as we move through our pregnancy. How do we manage and evaluate all the information coming at us?

One of the first things we need is a strategy for sifting through the deluge of information and picking out only what we need most. This may seem an impossible task, but we actually use these kinds of skills every day. For example, when we need toothpaste, we look for a product that will clean our teeth and freshen our breath. However, go into any supermarket, and you will be faced with racks and racks of options. But somehow you manage to sift through fresh mint, refreshing gels, whitening pastes, and all-in-one protection toothpastes to choose the toothpaste that meets your particular needs.

Now, choosing between a cesarean section and natural delivery may be slightly more challenging than choosing toothpaste, but the point is that we're quite capable of dealing with lots of information and shouldn't underestimate our ability to choose what is beneficial for us and for our growing babies. We have skills and strategies available for making choices according to our own values, purposes, and needs.

We will, however, have to let go of the myth that all information has equal value for all people. Choosing two or three trusted sources of information that we consistently refer to is one way of doing this. For example, you may find a book that seems to address your most pressing questions and a friend who is willing to share her own experiences with honesty and humor. These sources are worth more than a hundred arbitrary Web sites. But whatever you decide, there needs to be a connection between the advice you follow and your own values and understanding of yourself. It is possible to respect our own unique needs and preferences as well as others' as we seek out information that will contribute to our sense of serenity and well-being. Fiona came to the following conclusion:

> The best advice I ever received during my pregnancy was to ignore everyone's advice! The best advice I can give, as someone who was completely clueless, is to listen to your heart—your instincts won't let you down.

How are you managing to sift through all the bits of advice and information you're encountering?

Myth: It's Got to Be Perfect

> Perfection is the worst disease that ever afflicted the human mind.
> —Louis Fontanes[4]

During a break at work, I walked into the staff kitchen to find a heavily pregnant colleague chopping up fruit for her plain yogurt. "Wouldn't it be easier to use fruit yogurt?" I ventured.

"No," she said defensively. "They only put the discarded bits of fruit into fruit yogurt—there's hardly any goodness in it."

I couldn't dispute this, but what struck me was that someone so obviously tired, who had been on her feet all morning, would spend half of her ten-minute break taking the trouble to chop up "good fruit" for a "better" snack. Years later, as I watched her sixteen-year-old son play soccer, I wondered whether the "bad" yogurt would've made any difference!

Pregnancy, like any other life-changing experience, presents a new start, much like a New Year's resolution or a new job's challenges. It's an opportunity to try different approaches and fresh ways of doing things. *I might have failed in the past*, we think, *but I'm going to do this pregnancy thing right!* We commit ourselves to doing the things that will ensure a "good" pregnancy, an "effortless" birth, and a "healthy, happy" baby.

These words are in quotation marks because they are, of course, mythical. How can we judge what is good, healthy, and happy? What are the right things? And how do we measure their impact? There do seem to be some fairly obvious choices that are better for us and for our baby, such as eating sensibly, exercising, having regular checkups, and so on. However, the list seems to grow and change with each new generation, and the requirements become ever stricter—giving rise to the myth of the "perfect mother" and the "perfect pregnancy."

The myth of perfectionism invites us to believe that there is such a thing as the perfect mother-to-be and that I must be like her. The myth suggests, *If you do everything right, you will have a perfect baby—healthy, strong, and intelligent.*

Kim's account clearly expresses the effects of this myth:

> My pregnancy story is shot through with evidence of perfectionism. I investigated different birth options and decided I wanted to follow the natural birth route, with a midwife and no pain relief—this to me seemed the pinnacle of perfection. I also insisted that my husband feel the baby kicking at every opportunity and make conversation with my navel. He found waiting for the baby to kick infinitely tedious and only did it to humor me. This frustrated me immensely. How could we be the "perfect parents" and produce "perfect children" if he just wasn't prepared to play the game?

It's got to be perfect! Like all myths, the myth of the perfect mother who constantly strives to do things right seems to have some value and some foundation in truth, but when we look closer, it's actually an unrealistic demand that drains us and adds no real goodness to our lives.

The lie of perfectionism is that it can never be attained. Perfection is entirely subjective. Ask five people to describe their perfect night out, and you will get five different answers—so how will we ever know when we have achieved perfection? Perfectionism seduces us into wasting an enormous amount of energy striving for something that is ultimately, to borrow the words of Ecclesiastes 2:26 (NIV), "meaningless, a chasing after the wind."

How then do we deal with the myth of the perfect mother? One of the most important realizations we can come to is that we are loved just as we are. We need to hold on, in faith, to the awareness that who we are at the core is lovable and loved—by God and by those around us. We do not have to strive constantly to achieve in order to be accepted, because our worth does not depend on what we do but on who we are. We are who we are, and what we do is good enough.

As we accept this, we can begin to give ourselves the gift of permission. We can permit ourselves to do things our own way, to swim against the stream of perfectionism. Kim calls this "purposeful antiperfectionism." We can give ourselves permission to ignore pregnancy magazines, go to Irish dancing classes, or keep working as long as we want to. And we can give ourselves permission to draw a line and say, "That's good enough." We are able to choose from within the bounds of reason and according to our best judgment, but the point is to have the freedom to be ourselves rather than be dictated to by the rules of perfectionism.

Pregnancy offers us an opportunity to learn to be gentle with ourselves. Instead of pursuing the goal of perfectionism at great cost to ourselves and others, we can choose a different path that leads to self-care. Letting go of any habit is difficult, as we are used to certain patterns of thought and behavior, but it is liberating to make choices that nurture our bodies, souls, and minds. We can learn to pay attention to our needs and do what we can to look after ourselves. God loves us and takes care of us; God calls us to love and take care of ourselves as well.

Reflection

- How has perfectionism influenced your pregnancy?
- If your baby could speak to you right now, what do you think he or she would say?
- Is your baby's imagined voice similar to or different from the voices you hear around you?

The Deceptive Power of Myths

> During my pregnancy my joy was overshadowed by what people
> said or thought. I was torn between two worlds: what I felt and what
> I was "supposed" to feel. I never expressed my true feelings.
>
> —Lorraine

Myths have the power to influence how we think and feel about
pregnancy. First, they encourage us to assume that pregnancy is the
same for everybody, and that what works for one will work for all.
Second, when we accept the myths regarding pregnancy as the norm
and our own experiences of pregnancy do not fit neatly into the
"normal" mold, we begin to think that something is wrong with us.
We may even end up feeling disappointed or guilty for failing to
behave in an expected way.

Perhaps we do not feel blissfully happy all the time or are,
frankly, bored with reading about pregnancy-related issues. Perhaps, like Leigh, we sometimes have unexpected thoughts or feelings
that we feel sure no other pregnant mom ever had:

> As this baby grew within me, I felt invaded. There was something
> other than me inside me. There was something separate and yet
> a part of me—feeding off me, attached to me, moving inside me,
> and yet it was not me. The thought that sometimes came to mind,
> which I never confessed to another soul, so as not to appear weird
> or even bad, was: *What was the difference between this and cancer, a mass that
> grows and grows inside you, feeding off you for its own development?* When these
> thoughts came to mind, I felt trapped and repulsed by the very
> idea of being pregnant. I did not dwell on these thoughts and
> feelings, and fortunately they were fleeting.

Feelings like this can prevent us from finding authentic help and
support. We might be embarrassed or afraid to voice our concerns.
We may wonder what people would think if they knew how we really
feel. Women often deal with pressure and expectations by putting on
the mask of "all is well." We pretend wellness and confidence.

Because we believe that pregnancy and its related issues are things we should automatically know, or because we think that we should keep our feelings to ourselves, we may find ourselves withdrawing into a place of self-sufficiency. However, we risk becoming detached, isolated, and ultimately lonely.

Myths based on perfectionism only intensify loneliness because they're built on comparisons. They invite us to become competitive and judgmental, which only alienates us even further from the very women who could support and care for us, listen to and identify with us.

Here is how Lorraine and Kim described their struggles:

> The most negative aspect was the lack of support from older people who had had children. Child rearing and pregnancy were regarded as, "We all did this, so carry on and go through with it"—without any real emotional connection from the "schooled" in these things. Outwardly, I must've looked okay, but inwardly, I struggled with feelings of inadequacy and fears.
>
> —Lorraine

> None of my true feelings was for display in the public arena. My performance in public was shaped by the many popular and powerful ideas about expectant motherhood that circulate in my culture.
>
> —Kim

It is lonely to sit with feelings that run contrary to our own or others' expectations. Denise is afraid to talk to her husband about the fact that she wants a cesarean. She is beginning to resent her baby and doesn't know who to talk to about it. It's difficult to know who to talk to about such struggles because no one else seems to talk about the problems they had during pregnancy. As one woman put it, "You're supposed to be glad and grateful, so a conspiracy of silence exists." Studies indicate that nearly one in five pregnant women shows signs of depression, but many avoid discussing their symptoms with a doctor because they don't want to disappoint people.

In the midst of the loneliness, conflict, and stress lies the need for true mentoring. Expectant moms need guidance that helps and encourages, as opposed to information that just confuses. They also need to be able to express their feelings within a safe haven:

> A negative aspect of my pregnancy was my inexperience and ignorance and lack of real mentors. Negative counselors abounded, but I could have benefited from people who would listen to my concerns and be wise mentors.
>
> —Lisa

> It does help to have positive people around you who have been pregnant and who can encourage and support you and who take a genuine interest.
>
> —Gayle

When women enjoy genuine support, valuable advice, and a sense of inclusion, their experience of pregnancy can be transformed. Indeed, pregnancy can become a wonderful time of bonding, healing, and wholeness. The joy of being pregnant can transcend both societal pressures and our own sense of inadequacy.

We see this kind of support and solidarity in Luke's account of Mary and Elizabeth's relationship. When the angel appeared to Mary, he told her that her relative Elizabeth, who was older and had suffered infertility, was now pregnant. As soon as she could, Mary traveled to Judea to spend time with her. What a joyful reunion they must have had! Luke documents the beautiful praise songs these women sang about Mary's miracle baby, and the baby in Elizabeth's womb even leaped for joy.

Mary stayed with Elizabeth for three months, allowing both women to enjoy each other's company during their confinement: one in the early stages of pregnancy and the other nearing the birth of her baby. I imagine that they prayed and prepared together, thinking about how their lives would be when their babies were born, wondering what life held for each of their sons, and drawing strength from each other as they talked about their fears and hopes.

Theirs must have been an honest and intimate friendship that deepened over the months they shared together.

If we do find ourselves in a place of isolation during pregnancy, perhaps we can ask God to show us someone whom we can befriend. It may be someone in our prenatal class, someone who belongs to our circle of friends, or even an older woman whose wisdom gives us peace and reassurance. We can ask God to allow us to provide a safe place for each other where we can honestly share our journey through pregnancy.

Reflection

- What effect (if any) have myths about pregnancy had on your relationships?
- Which relationships help you to resist or ignore the myths?

The Liberating Power of Truth

> Do not conform any longer to the pattern of this world, but be transformed by the renewing of your mind. Then you will be able to test and approve what God's will is—his good, pleasing and perfect will.
>
> —Romans 12:2, NIV

Throughout this chapter we have seen how destructive myths can be. Myths parade as the truth and can distract us from life-giving truths. They can take us down a road of fear, loneliness, and confusion. The pursuit of truth is vastly different. Jesus said, "I am the way and the truth and the life" (John 14:6, NIV). This says to me that truth is not about chasing ideas and theories; it is about following a person whose lifestyle and teachings can transform us by renewing our minds and leading us into a richer and deeper experience of life.

In order to be transformed, however, we first need to be able to recognize the "pattern[s] of this world"—the myths that seem reasonable and helpful but lead us into confusion. Two little but extremely powerful words can signal that we are encountering a myth: *should* and *must*. These words need to set off warning bells in our minds because they are words of law, not freedom. They can trap us into ways of being that are not good for us. We need to challenge these words with questions like: Who says I must? Who will benefit if I do? How will this help me or my baby?

Another way to test whether an idea or belief is a myth is to ask how it makes us feel. Are we being lured into competition or comparison? Does it make us feel uneasy, inferior, or afraid? Do we feel confused? If we're just the slightest bit uncomfortable and can answer yes to any of these questions, we're probably staring a myth right in the face!

We need to discern which ideas have depth and substance that we can trust. The good news is that we do not have to do this discernment alone. Jesus called the Holy Spirit our Counselor and said, "When the Spirit of truth comes, he will guide you into all the truth" (John 16:13, NRSV). We have a counselor who can guide us toward truth according to God's values and principles. As we listen to that gentle but authoritative voice within us, we are paying attention to the counsel of the Holy Spirit.

Discerning myths for what they are is one thing, but we also need to determine what is true and helpful for us. As we journey through the nine months of pregnancy and into motherhood beyond, we need to be true to ourselves rather than living up to other people's expectations of us. If we are not accustomed to listening to ourselves, we may have trouble at first even knowing what we dream of or desire. Understanding what we want in our pregnancy and what we believe is a journey of discovery. It means listening to our reactions, spending time on our own and with God, asking ourselves the questions others have been asking, and coming up with answers that are true and beneficial for us.

Myths have power in times of uncertainty. Now, more than ever, we need to give ourselves space to find our own way and make our own decisions in our own time. Instead of judging ourselves harshly, we can applaud our efforts, decisions, and accomplishments. Instead of second-guessing ourselves, we can give ourselves permission to make independent choices and acknowledge our own strength of mind.

Although they couldn't entirely avoid the influence of myths, the following women made conscious decisions to think differently in the future. They recognized their limitations and strengths, gave themselves permission to rethink things, and allowed God to transform them:

> I am sad that we as women accept the invitation to enter into competition with other women rather than standing together in solidarity. Why did I? My only defense is that my worth then was completely wrapped up in being the best. That was my identity and my security.
>
> —Kim

> Looking back, I think that I would put less pressure on myself to appear as if I had everything together and would be more open to receiving advice and support. . . . God had to do a healing work in me so I could be at peace with whom he created me to be. . . . I realize how much guilt I've loaded on myself. Guilt is a thief that robs us of joy and delight.
>
> —Leigh

> I had to remind myself that I was valuable and that my own choices were acceptable. I've learned not to judge others on their choices or "performance" and not to compare myself or put myself under pressure. There isn't a "right" or "wrong," just an individual's choice.
>
> —Jenny

God's grace releases us from bondage to myths and false beliefs and from the need to strive and perform. As we listen to our counselor, the Holy Spirit; as we pay attention to the inner truth of our own being; and as we receive the gift of God's grace, our minds can be renewed and our spirits transformed so that we are no longer restricted to following the patterns of this world (Rom. 12:2). We can begin to redirect our thoughts to what is good and wholesome for ourselves, our baby, and our relationships.

> Whatever is true, whatever is noble, whatever is right, whatever is pure, whatever is lovely, whatever is admirable—if anything is excellent or praiseworthy—think about such things. . . . put it into practice. And the God of peace will be with you.
> —Philippians 4:8-9, NIV

Reflection

- In what area do you need the counsel of the Holy Spirit in order to discern what is true and beneficial for you?
- Take a few minutes to reflect on all that is "true," "pure," and "lovely" about being pregnant. Jot down everything that comes to mind. Look at your list regularly, adding new thoughts as they arise.

Invitation to Prayer

As we journey through pregnancy, at times inundated by information and struggling to discern truth, we need to know what and whom we can rely on. Ideas change, fashions change, medical knowledge changes, but God never changes.

When God spoke to Moses from the burning bush, Moses asked God to reveal God's name. God replied, "I AM WHO I AM" (Exod. 3:14, NIV). God is, was, and always will be the same. Our God is unshakable and always remains true to God's nature. Not only can we rely on this truth, but also we can center our lives on it.

In John's Gospel, Jesus identifies himself as the Son of God, having the same unchanging qualities as God, when he describes his nature and purpose in phrases beginning with the words "I am." Let's look at some ways in which Jesus describes himself:

"I am the bread of life." (John 6:35, NIV)
"I am the light of the world." (John 8:12, NIV)
"I am the gate for the sheep." (John 10:7, NIV)
"I am the good shepherd." (John 10:11, NIV)
"I am the way and the truth and the life." (John 14:6, NIV)
"I am the true vine." (John 15:1, NIV)

Which of Jesus' statements immediately captures your attention? Mark the statement, and perhaps even write it down.

Now find a quiet place and give yourself some time to listen to what God is saying to you through this statement. Don't think too hard or try to work it out; instead just be quiet in God's presence. This is a challenge for most of us in our times of prayer: being quiet without being distracted by our thoughts, plans, and other interruptions. Concentrating on a phrase from scripture can help us stay focused on God in prayer. As soon as we experience our minds wandering, we can gently bring ourselves back to the moment by reminding ourselves of our phrase.

During your time of quiet, hold on to your phrase from scripture by repeating it over and over in your mind. You are not memorizing it so much as savoring it. Say the words slowly. Allow their sweetness to melt and seep into your being, as if they were a piece of hard candy. Allow God's Spirit to speak to your spirit through the words.

You may find that as you repeat the phrase, one word stands out more strongly for you than the others. Trust that God has helped you to sift through all the words so that what remains is the word that is God's personal message to you. Whatever word you are left with, just sit with it, listening to its meaning for you.

After spending about ten to fifteen minutes on this prayer exercise, reflect on the words that have touched you. What did these words mean for you? Why do you think God has spoken these words into your life at this particular time? What have you learned about God from this time of prayer? What have you realized about yourself? What have you discovered about prayer?

Your phrase is now written onto your heart and can stay with you throughout the day or even the week. Each time you bring it to mind, it can nourish you. In this way Jesus truly is "the bread of life."

How would you like to end this time of prayer? Perhaps you could talk to God about what you have realized during this time and respond to the words you have received. You may respond with words of thanks and gratitude. Perhaps you want to ask God to guide you further or to reveal the meaning and purpose of these words more fully in your life. And perhaps there is no need for formal closure. God will be with you throughout the day, always ready to continue the conversation.

What's in this chapter?

*F*ear is an almost universal experience during pregnancy, yet few women feel free to talk about their fears. In this chapter we want to break the silence about women's fears and to acknowledge that fear is normal and can often be helpful—it is not sin or weakness. We also look at various strategies for managing fear.

- You are not alone
- What women fear during pregnancy
- To be afraid is to be human
- Acknowledge the fear
- Listen to your body
- Find the information you need
- Bring your fearful self home
- Share the fear with a trusted friend
- Pour out your heart to God
- Drag your thoughts away
- Go forward in spite of fear
- Invitation to Prayer: Enriching your image of God through scripture

5

FACING FEAR

So do not fear, for I am with you;
  do not be dismayed, for I am your God.
I will strengthen you and help you;
  I will uphold you with my righteous right hand.
. . . .
For I am the LORD, your God,
  who takes hold of your right hand
and says to you, Do not fear;
  I will help you.

—Isaiah 41:10, 13, NIV

Kim . . .

It started with one sharp twinge of pain in my lower abdomen. Immediately all my senses were alert, and my hands cradled my still-flat belly as I waited. It came again. I was aware of my breathing—too fast—and the pounding of my heart. I willed myself to calm down and breathe more deeply, focusing all my attention on identifying where the pain was coming from and what it meant. But the fear did not subside. It only intensified, rising in waves that threatened to overwhelm me. As the next pain began, I reached for the telephone.

I was ten weeks pregnant and alone in a hotel room, far away from home. The pains had begun as I settled down in bed. Although my doctor had assured me it was safe to travel, I had been concerned about a plane trip so early in my pregnancy. Now it seemed that my worst fears were being confirmed. I was sure that the pains meant I was losing my baby.

On the other end of the telephone, my husband was calm and rational. "I'm sure everything is fine. Where is the pain? What does the book say?" I took out my already dog-eared copy of *What to Expect When You're Expecting* and looked for questions about similar aches and pains. "Ligaments stretching," the book announced authoritatively. "Quite normal. No need to worry." My breathing eased, and I began to relax. I laughed a little with my husband about my panic, and we said good night.

Less than five minutes later I was gripped by another twinge of pain and a fresh onslaught of fear. No matter how I rationalized it, the clutch of dread in the pit of my stomach would not release its grip. I wrestled with my thoughts and with God—questioning, bargaining, and finally, pleading.

In tears, I phoned a friend and asked her to pray for me and my baby. She offered compassionate listening, sincere prayer, and a calm, reassuring presence until the panic subsided and I felt ready to face the night. But many hours passed before I could sleep. My prayers were heartfelt and doubt-filled, but somehow I was aware of an Other with me. I was not alone.

Even though the pains subsided that night, the feeling of anxiety remained until I had been safely at home for several days. And fear returned to me a number of times during my pregnancy with greater or lesser intensity.

My pregnancy fears did not only focus on the well-being of my baby. I worried that I would not be a good enough mother. I lay awake at night, thinking about poverty and war and aching for the world I was bringing my child into. I worried about the choices I was making in hospitals, birth options, and portable cribs. I was concerned about my body and whether I would ever get it back, as it grew and changed in ways I could not control.

And I felt alone in my fears. Apart from my night of fear in Cape Town, when I reached out to my husband and my friend, I bore much of my anxiety in silence. Some of my fears seemed too awful to be let out, while others were too trivial to acknowledge. Other pregnant women didn't seem to have the same fears, or at least those that I knew weren't talking about them—and neither did I.

In this chapter we want to break the silence about women's fears during pregnancy. We believe that honest conversation about fear helps put it into perspective and often reduces fear to manageable proportions. We also want to share a few strategies we have found helpful in managing fear.

You Are Not Alone

> Darkness is not the whole of the story—every pilgrimage has passages of loveliness and joy—but it is the part of the story most often left untold. When we finally escape the darkness and stumble into the light, it is tempting to tell others that our hope never flagged, to deny those long nights we spent cowering in fear.
> —Parker J. Palmer, *Let Your Life Speak*[1]

I hope that sharing my fears has reassured you that you are not the only one who has felt afraid during pregnancy. You may also feel relieved to know that at least one woman out there is far more neurotic than you!

Fear is an almost universal experience during pregnancy. Although our fears take different forms and focus on different aspects of the pregnancy, we all have fears. One study found that worry is one of the most common complaints of pregnancy. Worry affects more pregnant women than morning sickness and unusual food cravings combined.[2] And most pregnant women worry that they are worrying too much!

Many of our fears are rooted in a powerful instinct to protect our unborn babies. This is how Linda described it:

> I was amazed at how protective I became. I didn't want to travel with anyone who drove fast; I watched what I ate and didn't do strenuous exercise. I was petrified of doing something that might harm my precious cargo.

As our attachment to the little beings within us grows and we become increasingly aware of our responsibility as a mother-to-be, the desire to protect our babies can become quite intense. Our husbands and families may not fully understand why we feel so strongly, and we may not even be able to explain it ourselves. All we know is that we must do everything in our power to make sure no harm comes to our babies.

We need to acknowledge that this strong desire to protect is a gift from God. It is given to guide our actions and decisions, to help us nurture ourselves and our babies during the vulnerable time of pregnancy. Our God-given common sense and intuition are powerful inner resources that enable us to make sensible decisions for the care and protection of our unborn babies. They are not meant to be burdensome.

However, because research has made us aware of the dangers that a baby can be exposed to in utero, and because advertisements directed at mothers-to-be often play on their protective instincts, many women live through their pregnancies fearful that they may do the wrong thing. Then, as we have mentioned before, they may worry that even their worrying is harming the baby!

Reflection

- How have you experienced the instinct to protect your growing baby?
- What role have fear and worry played in your pregnancy up to now? How have they affected you?

What Women Fear During Pregnancy

> I was afraid in a general way that I would reject my child—that I simply would not like what turned up.
> —Margaret Hebblethwaite, *Motherhood and God* [3]

We included this section on fear not to give you more to worry about, but to reassure you that such concerns are common. Many other women are concerned about exactly the same things as you are.

Much of our anxiety during pregnancy seems to focus on our baby's well-being and our responsibility for nurturing and sustaining our baby's life. This is how these women described it:

> I was filled with anxiety and a million questions and fear—fear that something might go wrong. I worried myself sick every time the baby was quiet. I found myself drifting off into silent conversations with God, saying things like, "I promise, God, I will lead a good Christian life; just let my baby be healthy." Toward the end I felt so scared and unsure. I wish I had known that being afraid is normal.
>
> —Ursula

> And then there were the fears about what if there was something wrong with the baby. It's a useless and de-energizing kind of worry to lie awake wondering if your child will be born with some defect, or how you will cope or love it if it's not normal. But at some place deep inside me I also knew that God would give me whatever I needed to cope with what lay ahead, and my journey was to trust and abide in God.
>
> —Leigh

Pregnancy books, magazines, and Web sites seem to increasingly emphasize everything that moms-to-be need to do in order to ensure that their babies are calm, clever, confident, and creative. The idea that such outcomes can be controlled entirely by what mothers do during pregnancy places a huge and unnecessary burden on expectant moms. Gill struggled with guilt and fear throughout her pregnancy for supposedly having put her child at risk without even realizing it:

> I prayed for my child's health a lot. I was afraid that he wouldn't be normal, so I prayed for courage and strength to cope if things went wrong. My fears were about medication I had taken before I knew I was pregnant. I was so frightened that I had damaged my baby that I didn't mention this to anyone until Steven was safely born and I knew he was 100 percent okay.

Some mothers fear the birthing process and may grapple with anxiety about pain and even death. Jenny was afraid she would die and there would be no one to love her baby as much as she would have. Gayle, like many other women, was terrified of childbirth.

Another concern is our changing relationship with our spouses, friends, parents, and other children. Gill prayed fervently for her marriage. She worried about how she and her husband would cope as a couple if something was wrong with their baby. I remember also feeling concerned that things would not be the same anymore between my husband and me and wondering what our new circumstances would be like.

Pregnancy is also a time when we imagine what kind of parents we would like to be. Our fears may convince us that we have no hope of being a good enough parent to a vulnerable and dependent human being. This is how Fiona felt:

> When I was pregnant with my first baby, Luke, I was terrified about being a terrible mother. No one, including myself, could imagine me with a baby.

Fear seems constantly to ask the question, how will you cope? How will you cope if you have a miscarriage? if something is wrong with your baby? How will you cope with motherhood? Fear makes you question your strength and inner resources and suggests that they will never be sufficient should anything go wrong.

As happened with Heather, fear can provide you with endless possibilities of things that could go wrong:

> I was fearful of the unknown. Would I cope, would motherhood be what I expected, would I enjoy my baby?—and the list goes on. Would my baby be all right, was I eating correctly and enough so that my growing child would thrive? What if my child wasn't perfect—would I be able to cope with that, would I be angry with God, would I be able to handle what people would say or think if my child wasn't perfect?

Perhaps we need to beat fear at its own game by asking questions that focus on our strengths and resources: When did I cope well with a challenge or difficulty? How did I manage to do that? What does that say about me and my ability to cope with difficulties? What resources can I draw on during my pregnancy? Whom can I call on for help, if I should need it? What has been my experience of God in times of difficulty?

Reflection
Ask yourself the questions from the previous paragraph. Write your responses in your journal.

To Be Afraid Is to Be Human

> It is human to be afraid, and nothing to feel guilty about. It has nothing to do with sin, or with doing wrong. Fear is a feeling, and a sign that we are alive. . . . It is a signal that danger is near. We need to feel fear.
>
> —Grace Sheppard, *An Aspect of Fear* [4]

Fear is a normal and essential human response to any situation in which we feel the threat of danger, real or imagined. The awareness of danger triggers a complex physical reflex that floods our body with the energy we need to act quickly and decisively. This has been called the fight-or-flight reflex, as it allows us to confront or escape whatever is causing our fear. Fear is therefore essential to our survival as human beings.

However, as we grow up, we accumulate all sorts of ideas about fear from our culture and our families. We learn that fear is considered a weakness to be overcome, rather than a gift to be paid attention to. We learn that bravery and courage are applauded, while fear is ridiculed; courage is seen as the opposite of fear, rather than as a response arising from fear. We realize that fear is an uncomfortable feeling, and it makes others uneasy. In church we may have been taught that fear is somehow wrong or sinful and that the only proper response to fear is repentance.

We need to hear that even Jesus was afraid at times.

We need to hear that even Jesus was afraid at times. The Gospels give us a vivid picture of the fear and anguish Jesus endured in facing suffering, separation from God, and death. Mark 14:32-42 describes how, after sharing his last meal with his disciples, Jesus went out with them into the garden of Gethsemane to pray. A few of his closest disciples went on further with him, and Mark says "he began to be deeply distressed and troubled" and told his friends that his soul was "overwhelmed with sorrow to the point of death" (vv. 33–34, NIV).

I am sure that in the same circumstances, I would have clung to my friends, needing them to comfort and reassure me, to distract me from my fear. But Jesus did not. He left his friends behind and went on alone to pray through his fear, pouring out his heart to God in earnest prayer and pleading with God to spare him from the suffering that lay ahead.

His prayer was not polite, controlled, or detached. It was anguished and gut-wrenching. Drenched in perspiration that fell to the ground "like drops of blood" (Luke 22:44, NIV), Jesus' whole being gave voice to his turmoil. He was a mature, fully alive human being who knew his calling and purpose but at the same time felt the terror of facing brokenness and death. May we never be tempted to skim over Jesus' anguish. He didn't. He stayed with it until he was able to pray that amazing prayer of surrender: "Not my will, but yours be done" (Luke 22:42).

Pregnancy is a time of change and uncertainty, and fear is a natural response to a situation in which there are so many unknowns. So much is beyond our control. All we know for sure is that we have a new little life growing within us that must be sustained by our own bodies, and that our lives are about to change dramatically.

During pregnancy, as at all other times in our lives, fear alerts us to possible danger. For example, it is entirely appropriate to be afraid if you start to bleed during pregnancy, and to take action by seeing your doctor or midwife. However, fear becomes a problem when it is based on what *could* happen rather than what is happening. Fear of what might happen can destroy our peace of mind, deplete our inner resources, and isolate us from those closest to us.

Fear may be inevitable, but our response to it is not. A number of options are available to help reduce our levels of fear[5] and avoid getting stuck in the rut of worry. Jesus exemplifies one way to face fear: not to run away from it but to accept it, stay with it, and allow God to transform it into a resource for healing and growth.

In this chapter we invite you to accept that as a human being, you will experience fear. Acknowledging fear and listening to what it has to say can play a powerful role in managing your fears.

Reflection

- What ideas about fear did you grow up with?
- How does fear usually affect you?
- What do you usually do when you are afraid?

Acknowledge the Fear

> To fear is one thing. To let fear grab you by the tail and swing you around is another.
>
> —Katherine Paterson, *Jacob Have I Loved* [6]

Grace Sheppard, author of *An Aspect of Fear*, has struggled with fear for most of her life. The fears intensified as she got older, and her adult journey with fear has been difficult. However, the story of her journey has become a source of comfort and encouragement for others with similar struggles. She says that "acknowledging a specific fear helps us to be clear what we are fighting, and where the danger actually lies. It prevents us from being caught up in a world of un-reality." She encourages us to "isolate our fears before they isolate us," believing from her own long experience that "it will help, even if we just stop and acknowledge to ourselves that we are afraid." [7]

Have you ever found that the more you try to ignore a fear and hope it will go away, the stronger and more insistent it becomes?

Our awareness of our fears needs to come with compassion rather than with judgment.

Acknowledging our fears is a step forward on the journey into truth and freedom. If we don't admit them, our fears may begin to influence and dictate our behavior. They may end up driving, controlling, and even possessing us.

It takes a great deal of courage to acknowledge fear, as many of us are afraid of fear itself. We may be afraid that fear will overwhelm us if we even admit that it is there. We may be particularly afraid of those fears that we consider less acceptable or respectable. We need to hear again that fear is neither right nor wrong, good nor bad; it just is. Our awareness of our fears needs to come with compassion rather than with judgment.

Grace Sheppard found that facing the truth allowed her to stop pretending, which in turn enabled her to relate to others more deeply. She writes that acknowledging fear was like switching on the light in a dark room that she had imagined to be full of bogeymen.[8]

Reflection

What might you see if you switched on the light in your own dark room full of bogeymen?

Listen to Your Body

> Didn't you realize that your body is a sacred place, the place of the Holy Spirit?
>
> —I Corinthians 6:19, *The Message*

Because fear triggers a bodily response, the body is a good place to start in learning to manage fear. Many of us are not used to listening to our bodies; we see them as obstacles to overcome rather than as friends that we need to pay attention to. We may have learned over the years to ignore or deny the distress signals that our bodies send us, as these might interfere with our plans and agendas or remind us of our vulnerability.

The very physicality of pregnancy is an invitation to come home to our bodies and make peace with our human forms. One way to do this is to simply become more aware of our bodies, how they feel and how they move. As we learn to listen to our bodies, we can begin to detect their signals of pleasure and of distress. Our bodies reflect a wide range of emotions, and we can often understand what we are really feeling by paying attention to our bodies.

When a fear response is triggered in your brain, the brain instantly sends a message to your body, which responds in various ways: your heart may pound; your muscles may tense; and your palms, neck, and forehead may perspire. Fear may express itself in a tight jaw, stiff shoulders, or a clenched fist. I usually find it more difficult to breathe deeply or swallow when I am afraid, and I feel a tightness in my stomach.

Becoming aware of how fear is expressed in our bodies is the first step to managing fear. We can then instruct our bodies to help us by consciously beginning to relax the tense places. We can take slow, deliberate breaths to regulate our breathing. Our bodies and minds are in a cooperative relationship, so, as we begin to express calmness through our bodies, we also send a message to our minds and emotions that all is well, and we begin to feel less anxious. Our bodies have much to teach us about fear and how to manage it, if we just take the time to listen.

Reflection

- Spend a few minutes focusing on your breathing. Don't try to regulate it; just be aware of what happens in your body as you breathe in and breathe out.
- What are you aware of in your body right now?
- If your body could speak to you now, what do you think it might say?

Find the Information You Need

> Nothing in life is to be feared. It is only to be understood.
> —Marie Curie, French chemist and physicist

The right information at the right time can be a useful antidote to many of our pregnancy fears. Most of our fears arise because we don't understand the strange new sensations in our bodies, and we don't know what to expect through each phase of pregnancy. Armed with the facts about what is known, we may feel less daunted by the unknowns. Although each pregnancy is unique, we can learn a great deal from medical science and the experience of other mothers to guide us through the decisions we will face during our pregnancy.

However, as we discussed in "Recognizing Myths," information can be a two-edged sword. Leigh describes her search for information during her first pregnancy as follows:

> I did what many modern mothers do best when they need reassurance and guidance—I read. I read about the developmental stages of the baby, about the process and progress of pregnancy, about birth and ways of giving birth. The information was in a sense reassuring, just because I now felt better informed, but it was also mind-boggling and frightening with so many new terms and decisions I was going to have to make about things I really was completely unsure of. Fortunately, time was on my side. I had the several months of pregnancy to reread and mull over these things, and I at least became more familiar with the language and the procedures.

Childbirth education classes usually provide us with reliable information in bite-sized chunks and have been found to significantly reduce levels of fear for most pregnant women (and their spouses). In these classes you can ask questions, learn specific techniques for managing fear and pain during childbirth, and meet other couples who are going through the same life experience. Many strong friendships are forged during such classes, friendships that continue to provide support and companionship for years after the babies are born. The classes will be most helpful if they feel like a safe space where you can be honest, without fear of judgment or criticism.

I found the classes empowering, and I believe they helped me face childbirth with a sense of calm and confidence in my ability to cope. This is not true for all women. Some women find the classes frightening, particularly when they are expected to watch graphic videos detailing various women's experiences in labor and birth. For many, ignorance in this regard is indeed bliss, and they would prefer to go into childbirth with no expectations, guided by their

Each expectant mom needs to seek out the information she needs, in a format she relates to, in order to address her particular concerns about the pregnancy and birth. And if information makes you nervous, for heaven's sake, put your feet up and read a good novel instead!

Reflection

- For you, does information tend to grow fear or shrink it?
- What information do you feel you need at this time?

Bring Your Fearful Self Home

> Jesus dwells in your fearful, never fully received self. . . . Where you are most human, most yourself, weakest, there Jesus lives. Bringing your fearful self home is bringing Jesus home.
> —Henri J. M. Nouwen, *The Inner Voice of Love* [9]

Have you ever felt pulled in different directions by all the voices in your head when you had a decision to make? One part of you says this while another part says that. A number of Christian authors have described our inner conflicts and inconsistencies as the result of many different "selves" or "voices" that coexist within us and make up who we are.[10] This metaphor invites us to see ourselves not as having one single, consistent self but as being made up of many different selves with a variety of dreams, priorities, and agendas.

During my pregnancies I became aware of a number of new selves that I had not encountered before: my nurturing self; my fierce mother-wolf, protective self; my sensual self. But one of the selves I tried to ignore and run away from for much of my pregnancy was my fearful self.

In his book *Signposts to Spirituality*, Trevor Hudson suggests that there is a tendency, particularly in Christian circles, to acknowledge only our acceptable or good selves, such as our patient self, our self-sacrificing self, and so on. Those selves we consider unacceptable, such as our fearful or angry self, are usually either neglected or rejected. The result is a tragic situation where "large tracts of our inner life are prevented from experiencing God's transforming friendship."[11]

When we take the time to meet with our fearful self and listen to her story, she can tell us a lot about what we are really afraid of and what we really need. We are then able to bring our fears and needs into the light of God's love and grace. I discovered this when I was pregnant with my first daughter, Caydn.

During this first pregnancy, fear was never far away, and the question that tormented me most often was: *Will my baby be normal?* On the surface, this is an ordinary fear shared by millions of mothers-to-be around the world. But was there more to it than that? I was amazed by what I discovered when I let my fearful self speak.

Three and a half years before becoming pregnant with Caydn, I was hospitalized while I struggled to reclaim my life from anorexia and bulimia. This slow and torturous process continued for years after my discharge from the hospital. My body, which had stopped ovulating, did not start functioning properly again even when my weight was at a healthy level. I sought help from fertility specialists over a period of two years with no success before feeling "led"—both by my emotional exhaustion and a scripture verse that spoke deeply to me—to stop the treatment and trust God for the child I so desperately wanted.

About nine months later, I had my first period in five years, and hope grew. After I had three periods, Dave and I felt that we could try the fertility treatment one more time. This time it was successful, and I conceived.

But then I began to worry: *Will my baby be normal?* I eventually shared this fear with a wise friend who encouraged me to listen to it more closely. What I discovered was that behind the normal or acceptable fear lay a deep mistrust and fear of God. Guilt led me to believe that I had interfered with God's work by requesting medical help and had spoiled what could have been a perfect or miraculous conception. I was afraid that God might punish my lack of faith and patience by giving me a less-than-perfect baby.

It was not easy to face these thoughts and fears or to sit with my fearful self without judgment, but as I listened, I recognized for the first time just how distorted and unhealthy my image of God had become. I also realized how much of my fear was about the need for things to be perfect. Fear of being blamed if my baby was deformed in some way also showed itself, as did the fear of being unable to cope with pain. I also heard my sadness at the abuse my body had suffered and my concern for the long-term implications of that abuse for myself and for my baby.

What I heard as I listened to my fear proved to be a rich resource for reflection, prayer, and growth during my pregnancy. Fear did not disappear, but I now realized that it signaled distress in my inner world that deserved attention.

Reflection

- How do you respond to the idea that we are made up of many selves?
- If you listened to your fearful self right now, what do you think it would say to you?

Share the Fear with a Trusted Friend

What we hunger for perhaps more than anything else is to be known in our full humanness, and yet that is often just what we also fear more than anything else. It is important to tell at least from time to time the secret of who we truly and fully are . . .

because otherwise we run the risk of losing track of who we truly and fully are and little by little come to accept instead the highly edited version which we put forth in hope that the world will find it more acceptable than the real thing.

—Frederick Buechner, *Telling Secrets*[12]

Sharing our fears can be risky business. It's not often done in a culture that does not tolerate weakness and instead pursues the ideals (idols?) of independence, self-sufficiency, control, and success. But is this the culture of the kingdom of God?

My understanding of scripture tells me that the kingdom is more about dependence on God than about independence, more about acknowledging our limitations than about self-sufficiency, more about surrender than control, and more about fruitfulness than success.[13] Sharing our brokenness with another person fosters intimacy and community. It also somehow opens up new possibilities for healing and release. This is certainly what happened when I shared my fears for my baby with my friend, as I described in the previous section.

However, my life experience has also taught me that there is wisdom in carefully selecting the person with whom I will share my heart. I make sure that I find someone who listens well—someone in whom I have recognized wisdom, compassion, and a deep respect for other people's stories. I tend to avoid sharing deeply with people who jump in with advice and easy answers or who want to immediately apply scripture or prayer like a Band-Aid to my fears.

I encourage you to continue praying and seeking until you find a faithful, compassionate companion for the journey through pregnancy and the years to come. The Celts called such a person a "soul friend." Margaret Silf says that a soul friend needs no special qualifications except that he or she should be a person of prayer, someone who takes seriously his or her spiritual journey, and someone who loves God.[14] Think of the people you know who fit this description.

Reflection

- What qualities would you look for in a soul friend?
- How could you go about developing such a friendship if you don't have one already?

Pour Out Your Heart to God

> Do not be anxious about anything, but in everything, by prayer and petition, with thanksgiving, present your requests to God. And the peace of God, which transcends all understanding, will guard your hearts and your minds in Christ Jesus.
>
> —Philippians 4:6-7, NIV

> I would pray until the fear abated. I would pray until I had peace.
>
> —Jenny

I mentioned earlier the vivid description in scripture of the fear Jesus experienced the night before he died. He literally poured out his heart to God, begging God to change the course of his life. What touches me very deeply about Jesus' prayer is its complete honesty; Jesus does not pretend to be in a better place than he is. And yet, somehow, through the time of prayer, he is changed. God journeys with him through the anguish until he is able to choose the way of trust and surrender.

Following Jesus' way seems to require that I be real with God about all of my life and that I grapple with pain and with all of my selves until I reach the point of surrender. This is certainly what the psalmists seem to do. Whenever I read the Psalms, I am struck by how unashamedly real the psalmists were about their thoughts and feelings, holding nothing back and apparently unafraid that God or others would disapprove. They poured out their fears and dreams to a God they clearly believed was listening. Yet, however bad they felt and however awful their circumstances, they would come to a place of trust in the God whose help they had known in the past and anticipated in the future.

Following the psalmists' example, I began to write down prayers that previously I had not even allowed my heart to whisper. I find that writing slows my racing mind and helps me focus my thoughts. This practice has become a vital aspect of my prayer life, and often my written prayers reveal thoughts and feelings that I had not even been aware of.

I have found that a new sense of serenity comes whenever I clear out some of the stuff that is cluttering my head and heart and look at it with God in this way. It seems to leave an inner space in which I can be still and wait with God, without needing to speak, just listening.

And what am I listening for in the stillness of my heart? In *Bread for the Journey*, Henri J. M. Nouwen says that underneath all the noisy voices, within and outside us, that vie for our attention, "there is a still small voice that says: 'You are my Beloved, my favour rests on you.' That's the voice we need most of all to hear."[15] In *Life of the Beloved*, Nouwen writes, "Every time you listen with great attentiveness to the voice that calls you the Beloved, you will discover within yourself a desire to hear that voice longer and more deeply."[16] The still, small voice of love often seems to speak into our fears with a word, picture, or symbol of hope and healing. First John 4:18 says that "perfect love drives out fear" (NIV). As we spend time in humble communion with God, the divine whisper of love can tame even our wildest fears.

Leigh tells in the next chapter, "Encountering God," how God spoke comfort, strength, and reassurance to her through a verse of scripture that calmed her fears during her difficult second pregnancy. Gayle, on the other hand, was given a beautiful picture that reassured her that she was not alone as she faced what was for her the terrifying prospect of giving birth:

> I had immense fear of giving birth. It was quite overwhelming.
> Then the Lord gave me a picture: I was standing on some rocks,

unable to jump from one rock over to another. Then I saw Jesus standing on the other side, and then I knew that he'd be waiting on the other side—that he'd be there, waiting for me at the birth.

Reflection

- Dip into the book of Psalms and read whichever psalms catch your attention. Using the structure of the Psalms as a guide-line, write your own psalm, pouring out your heart to God.
- In what situations have you received a message of comfort? When have you been "given" a scripture or image at just the right time? Describe these experiences in your journal.

Drag Your Thoughts Away

Drag your thoughts away from your troubles by the ears, by the heels, or any other way, so you manage it.

—Mark Twain [17]

The difference between fear and worry lies in the realm of choice. Fear is an automatic physiological response to a situation in which we feel threatened. Worry, on the other hand, is a conscious straying of our thoughts to a particular situation that troubles us. While fear energizes and primes us for action, worry spins its wheels endlessly without moving forward, draining us of all energy and creativity. Yet, worry is actually something we can control—we can choose the object of our thoughts.

Mark Twain's suggestion that we "drag our thoughts away" from those things that trouble us acknowledges the fact that choosing not to worry takes a lot of effort. It is not a simple matter and requires commitment and self-discipline. But it is possible.

Matthew's Gospel records Jesus' teachings about the futility of worry. Jesus points to the birds of the air and the lilies of the field, which live in the moment, do no strategic planning or forecasting or saving for a rainy day, and yet they are provided for. He reminds us that each day holds its own troubles—and blessings. Worry about tomorrow gets in the way of living today to the fullest.

Many mothers have realized this in retrospect and have felt sad that they didn't "drag their thoughts away" more often during pregnancy.

> Take each day and stage as it comes. Nine months sounds like such a long time, and then it's over in a flash. Take time to lie back and enjoy the miracle.
>
> —Kim V.

> Don't rush the pregnancy—enjoy each day, each movement; indulge in the thought of holding your child, and don't waste too much energy on the "what ifs?" I wanted to control my pregnancy, but you can't do that. God can't build your puzzle unless you give him all the pieces.
>
> —Ursula

> Enjoy each moment and live in "the new." Don't get caught up in the planning only; enjoy the new life.
>
> —Lorraine

No foolproof formula exists for avoiding worry, but scripture offers a few suggestions. The first is to become more aware of everything in our lives for which we are grateful—and to thank God for each one (1 Thess. 5:18). And the second is to keep returning our thoughts to that which is life-giving and hope-filled (Deut. 30:19-20; Phil. 4:8).

Reflection

- What effective strategies have you found for "dragging your thoughts away" from a place you didn't want them to be?
- Have you ever experimented with keeping a gratitude journal? What happened?

Go Forward in Spite of Fear

> Courage doesn't always roar. Sometimes courage is the quiet
> voice at the end of the day saying, "I will try again tomorrow."
> —Mary Anne Radmacher, writer and artist[18]

Fear offers each of us the opportunity to demonstrate courage.
After all, we don't need courage unless we're afraid. Courage does
not mean that we deny or avoid the fear. Author Erica Jong says, "I
have accepted fear as a part of life, specifically the fear of change, the
fear of the unknown, and I have gone
ahead despite the pounding in the heart
that says: turn back."[19] This is courage.

*It takes courage
to carry a baby in
your womb and to
bring a child into
the world.*

Courage means different things to
each of us at different times. Sometimes it
is courageous to take action, and sometimes it is courageous to withdraw. Perhaps courage for you means making an
appointment for an amniocentesis, or
perhaps it means canceling the appoint-
ment you made in fear. For one woman it may be courageous to buy
a book and read to get the information she needs. For another it
may be courageous to stop reading.

Most of the stories in this chapter are stories of courage. It takes
courage to carry a baby in your womb and to bring a child into the
world. It takes courage to acknowledge your fears and listen to them.
It takes courage to seek out the information that you both desire and
are afraid of hearing and to make decisions. It takes courage to share
your fears with God and others, and it takes courage to listen for
God's voice. It takes courage to have faith and choose hope. It takes
courage to live.

Where does this courage come from? The lion in *The Wizard of Oz*
discovered that courage was there all along, although he hadn't realized it. Grace Sheppard says, "Courage is waiting for us to take hold
of it. It is nearer when we are in touch with ourselves, when we know

what we want."[20] It may also be nearer when we are in touch with others and with God. The loving presence of another or an Other may give us the courage and strength we need. The seed of courage often looks remarkably like faith, like hope, and sometimes even like laughter. Sometimes we find the courage we need when we stop taking life—and ourselves—so seriously and take the risk of dancing with the wind rather than trying to direct it.

Reflection

- What does courage mean for you right now?
- Where does your courage come from?

Invitation to Prayer

The fear that underlies many of our fears is a fear of God. If we're honest, many of us have a mental picture of a God we are not sure can be trusted. God may seem to be a temperamental tyrant who decides our fate on a whim, or a weak and ineffectual nice being who has no real say over what happens in our lives. The only way to begin to heal our image of God is to take the risk of looking deeply into God's face and meeting God's eyes. This may seem impossible because we cannot see God. In fact, especially as we face our fears, God may seem very far away. But God, in grace and love, did become visible and accessible to us in Jesus. And Jesus reveals to us what God is really like.

In this time of prayer we will spend time looking at different pictures of Jesus revealed to us in the Gospel stories. As we watch how Jesus lived and related to people, we hope to discover a picture of God that draws us closer to God and speaks to us in our fears.

As you read through each of these descriptions of Jesus, take some time to see the picture in your mind. Then ask yourself: What does this picture of Jesus tell me about the character of God? How does this picture help me face my fears during pregnancy?

Image 1 (Luke 2:6-7)

> While they were there, the time came for the baby to be born, and she gave birth to her firstborn, a son. She wrapped him in cloths and placed him in a manger, because there was no room for them in the inn. (NIV)

Jesus is a newborn—face wrinkled, hair matted, and probably still smeared with blood. Snugly wrapped in strips of cloth, he lies nestled in a bed of straw. He is sleeping, and you can see his chest rising and falling ever so slightly. He is the image of every baby—so utterly at peace in sleep and yet so tiny, helpless, and vulnerable.

Image 2 (John 4:1-26)

> Jesus said to her, "Everyone who drinks of this water will be thirsty again, but those who drink of the water that I will give them will never be thirsty. The water that I will give will become in them a spring of water gushing up to eternal life." (vv. 13-14, NRSV)

Jesus, tired and thirsty, sits on the edge of a desert well in the midday heat. A Samaritan woman comes to draw water, and Jesus asks her for a drink, breaking several religious and cultural laws in one gesture. They begin a conversation in which he acknowledges the pain and messiness of her life. He offers her the water of God's Spirit, which will quench the deep thirsting of her soul.

Image 3 (Luke 7:11-17)

> When the Lord saw her, his heart went out to her and he said, "Don't cry." (v. 13, NIV)

Jesus notices a funeral procession moving slowly along the road, carrying the body of a young man. Following behind is a widow mourning her only son, crying and wailing at the loss of her precious child. Jesus, moved with compassion, reaches out to comfort her, and he revives her son, giving her back what she loves and needs most. The people respond in awe and praise, "God has come to help his people" (v. 16, NIV).

Image 4 (Luke 18:15-17)

> [Jesus said] "Let the little children come to me, and do not hinder them, for the kingdom of God belongs to such as these." (v. 16, NIV)

People must have made constant demands on Jesus. The disciples, wanting to protect Jesus from being bothered by women bringing their children to him to be blessed, turn the women and children away. But Jesus stops the disciples. He calls for the children to be brought to him, and children perch on his lap, are held in his arms, and sit at his feet. He touches and blesses them, but more than that, he holds up children as treasured examples of the humility, openness, and trust required to enter God's kingdom.

As you spent time with each of these images, which one had the most meaning for you? What draws you to this particular image? What do you think God is saying to you about facing your fears? What, if anything, has changed about your image of God? Perhaps you might end your time of prayer by asking God to fill you with the peace and power that comes through the Holy Spirit.

What's in this chapter?

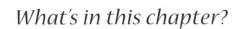

*P*regnancy offers a unique opportunity to encounter God in a new way. In this chapter we
share the stories of various women's experiences of God
during pregnancy. We deal with these topics:

- Encountering God through good and bad times
- Encountering God as Creator
- Encountering God as Love
- Encountering God as Mother
- Encountering God as Protector and Healer
- Encountering God as Mystery
- Encountering God with gratitude
- Invitation to Prayer: Praying life and blessing for
  our babies

6

ENCOUNTERING GOD

God of life, you labor with all creation
to bring forth the holy.
Be with me, breathe through me
as I ponder the life I am fashioning.

—Jan L. Richardson, *Sacred Journeys*

Leigh . . .

Kim loves to tell the story of how she encountered the God of resurrection and life unexpectedly one precious Easter weekend—the weekend she discovered she was pregnant after struggling for years with infertility. The day after she got the news was Easter. She and her husband attended a sunrise service in their local park, but she didn't hear a word of the sermon:

> I hugged the news to myself, reveling in my inner Easter. I remember so clearly a sense of God's being with me in a new way. It was a resurrection moment for me as I embraced the new life that had been called forth from the pain and uncertainty of the years gone by.

Kim had had her fair share of Good Fridays, but just as God breathed life into death and hope into despair on that miraculous day when Jesus was raised to life, so God breathed new life and hope into Kim through the news of her pregnancy. We all have our own "inner Easters" in different ways and at different times. Pregnancy can be one of those times.

During pregnancy we have the privilege of encountering God in a new and vital way. Pregnancy becomes what in Celtic terms is called a "thin place"—where the dividing line between this world and the spiritual realm stretches to the point that there is hardly a barrier between the two. A thin place is where people begin to "search for deeper meaning, presence and wholeness to life."[1] Pregnancy certainly seems to be such a place, inviting us to reflect on the meaning of our lives from a fresh perspective, to reach out to God and to encounter the One who brings meaning, presence, and wholeness into our lives.

Eve vividly describes how in the "thin place" of pregnancy she met God in a powerful way:

> My experience of God throughout my pregnancy was awesome. I experienced anew so many facets of God's character that became so real to me—God the creator, God the One abounding in love, God the giver of amazing grace, and God who is ever faithful!

Eve reminds us that there are many aspects to God's character, and different aspects become more real and meaningful to us at different times. Many women relate especially to God as creator and nurturer during pregnancy through their sense of participating with God in the miraculous act of creation. Others become particularly aware of God's love and grace. We can also meet God as healer and protector as we become aware of our own vulnerability and woundedness. Above all, pregnancy is an opportunity to acknowledge that God remains Mystery, beyond the reach of our words, our understanding, and our control.

This chapter explores various facets of God's nature that women have encountered during their pregnancies. We also look at our responses to the God who meets us in this "thin place." Each of our responses will be unique, but perhaps the most appropriate one is that of gratitude and worship.

Reflection

How have you encountered God in your pregnancy so far?

Encountering God through the Worst and Best of Times

> I fled Him, down the nights and down the days;
>   I fled Him, down the arches of the years;
> I fled Him, down the labyrinthine ways
>   Of my own mind; and in the midst of tears
> . . . .
> From those strong Feet that followed, followed after.
>   But with unhurrying chase,
>   And unperturbèd pace,
> Deliberate speed, majestic instancy,
>   They beat—and a Voice beat
>   More instant than the Feet . . .
>   —Francis Thompson, "The Hound of Heaven" [2]

Megan was twenty years old and single when she became pregnant the first time. This devastated her, as she had grown up in a strict but loving home that held to high Christian morals. She felt she had let her family down, and she couldn't bear the thought of disappointing them. She describes her reaction:

> I was petrified by the thought of being pregnant and never went for an official test; I suppose I was hoping that if I never heard the words "Your test is positive," it wouldn't actually be true. As I had already planned to travel overseas for a working holiday, I made

the decision to continue with that plan. I wouldn't have to tell anyone of my pregnancy; I would put the baby up for adoption and come home again with no one having to be hurt or upset by my indiscretion.

So Megan spent the remainder of her pregnancy alone in London, far from anyone she knew and loved, just waiting for the baby to born. Besides the loneliness, what weighed heavily on her was the temptation to get rid of her "problem" altogether by having an abortion:

> I was so afraid that I would give in to the temptation of having an abortion. I did not trust myself at all. In London every tube and train station was covered with posters advertising free abortions. I would not sleep at night until I was past the stage that an abortion is possible. It was almost like there was a war going on inside me. An abortion would have meant a quick end and an opportunity for me to get on with my life. But I also knew that I did not want to go down that road. I really did not trust myself to make the right decision and so was afraid right up until I did not have the option any longer.

Given all this, it is not surprising that Megan felt far from God:

> I did not include God in any part of my pregnancy. I had decided to cope with it on my own, and I guess I knew that if I had sought God, he would have led me to handle it differently. I was so determined to do it my way that I refused to let anyone in— even God.

However, while God lets us make our own choices, our Maker does not leave us alone, and even in this dark place there were times when Megan recognized God's presence with her. First she felt God moving her heart to love the baby growing inside her despite her own determination not to:

> I could not deny that God was beginning to knit my heart with that of my unborn baby.

God also reassured Megan of God's love and presence with her in simple ways that she recognized:

> It was obvious that God was near me, especially toward the end. I hardly ever prayed and never read my Bible, but God showed himself to me in other ways. I was aware of his love for me and his acceptance of me. When the wind blew on my face, I felt like it was my Father saying, "It's all going to be okay." Only now when I look back do I see how God had me in the palm of his hand all along, and how he began to form a love between mother and child long before the child was born.

Megan had a traumatic birth experience, alone in a hospital far from home, with less-than-sympathetic support from the hospital staff. However, the work God had begun in her spirit during her pregnancy continued after the birth of her daughter. Two days after the baby was born, Megan phoned the father of her baby, who, after the shock had worn off somewhat, flew to London, collected Megan and their newborn baby, and brought them both back home.

Megan's story continues after she married her baby's father, had a second baby some time later, and then came to a deeper faith in God. All these factors profoundly influenced how she felt about her third pregnancy:

> My husband and I had always planned to have four children, so when I got pregnant for the third time we rejoiced and celebrated. The timing was perfect, and we were in a good place relationally, spiritually, and financially.

This pregnancy became a healing journey for Megan and her husband and seemed to counteract every painful moment of her first pregnancy. First, instead of feeling afraid and lost, Megan experienced a sense of security and purpose in this pregnancy:

> Unlike with either of my other pregnancies, I was very aware of the fact that God had created me, that he had created my baby, that one of my purposes in this life was to carry and have

children, and so I was in the perfect will of God. It was a very secure place to be. We knew that God was leading us in every decision we made.

Second, instead of blocking God out, Megan welcomed God's involvement in her pregnancy and expressed a deep gratitude for everything God was doing in and around them:

Because we had a closer relationship with God during this pregnancy, we were more aware of the little things that he was doing, like causing me to want our home to be just right for our baby. He brought a gentleness into our hearts. We felt safe, secure, and totally surrounded by his love.

God also ensured that Megan would not be alone during this pregnancy. Notice in the following excerpt how many people surrounded and supported her:

I loved the closeness I felt between my husband and me during this time. My closest friend became pregnant at the same time as me, so that was also great fun—comparing notes and sharing feelings. Another exciting thing was having two children already who were old enough to understand what was happening and to share in the excitement of the development of *our* new baby.

Finally Megan had a birth experience that was as calm and wonderful as her first was not. She and her husband decided to have the baby at home. While friends and family prayed and a warm and caring professional midwife stood by them, Megan gave birth to a healthy little boy:

We had music playing in the background and a couple of women friends with us to pray and support us. Whenever I started to feel pain, my husband prayed, and the pain instantly left. It was so obvious that one of the women actually asked why the contractions had stopped. The midwife replied that they hadn't stopped, but they were simply not painful, so you couldn't recognize them by my breathing. If I didn't know better, I would have said that God had left the whole world to be with my family and me that day.

Reflection

- How do you respond to Megan's story?
- What does her story say to you about God?

Encountering God as Creator

In all her newness
I watch her discover each part
and pray that eye
and ear
and hand may always be open
to know the one who fashioned them.
—Jan L. Richardson, *Sacred Journeys* [3]

God is the source of life. This may seem like an obvious statement, but it becomes very real when we assume our role as participants with God in creating a new life. This is how Kim expressed it in her journal when she became pregnant:

THANK YOU! THANK YOU! THANK YOU! . . . I am still finding it difficult to take it in—there is a baby, a real whole person, growing inside me! Created, designed, planned, given life by God—and God alone.

Every day evidence of life surrounds us: in nature, in people, in activity, even in our very breathing, but we sometimes take it for granted. One of the gifts of pregnancy is that every nudge from inside us reminds us that life is precious and indeed miraculous. It is therefore not surprising that pregnancy is a time when many women are more aware of the one true origin of this life and all life—God as Creator.

I remember experiencing a kind of aching wonder, where words are almost impossible, when I contemplated the development of each of my babies as they grew within me. Through books and my imagination, I followed the development of the fetus from its few little cells to something so amazingly complex and intricate that it was indeed a miracle.

But it wasn't until I felt that first little flutter, that ripple of movement inside me, that I connected what I was imagining with my own baby growing inside me. When I felt that movement, it brought me to the reality of what this was about. A living creature was forming within me. I was utterly amazed at this knowledge. I was in awe of the fact that I was bearing a live, growing, human being and that I was participating with God in this creative process. In the face of such mystery and miracle, sometimes all you can do is sit in hushed wonder.

The Bible opens with the phrase "In the beginning God created" (Gen. 1:1, NIV). We cannot underestimate the power of these words. God's first act, the first expression of God's essence and being, was to create. And our first introduction to God names God as Creator. For me, this word *create* is so rich with meaning. It implies imagination, planning, design, artistry, molding, building, fashioning, changing, working with passion and delight, and making something beautiful, with a purpose.

The psalm writer feels moved to worship as he describes what it means for him to know God as his creator:

> For you created my inmost being;
>   you knit me together in my mother's womb.
> I praise you because I am fearfully and wonderfully made;
>   your works are wonderful,
>   I know that full well.
>
> —Psalm 139:13-14, NIV

When Eve realized she was pregnant with twins, she was deeply moved by a fresh awareness of God's gift of creation, much like the psalmist. This became very real for her when she saw her babies' heartbeats on the ultrasound screen:

> There are no words to describe the feelings of seeing the heartbeats of two perfectly formed babies on the sonar screen—I was astounded by the majesty of God the Creator. Just knowing that I was given the amazing opportunity to carry and raise two babies also reminded me of God's love for me.

Other women have felt the same sense of wonder and joy, even when only one heartbeat appears on the ultrasound:

> I experienced the wonder of new life and a special sense of God's creation. For me, God's creation has always been the way to get close to God, and when the wonder of that new life is within your body, you can't help but marvel.
>
> —Caroline

> I remember reading with my husband and looking at pictures as we went along: six weeks, ten weeks, fifteen weeks, and thinking how awesome God is to have created something so spectacular. I remember feeling blown away by this miracle, and how God had made me able to carry this baby, grow it, nurture it—all inside my body—and then to birth it.
>
> —Janine

> I was full of awe at the miracle God had created in me. The miracle of the baby's development filled me with wonder at the power of the Creator. I was amazed at how people could have children and not believe in God, because the whole experience of pregnancy demonstrated for me the miracle of creation.
>
> —Janet

Creation becomes very real and personal when it is happening inside us! As we wonder at God's creation, we often feel compelled to respond in the only way creatures know how—with worship.

There are many expressions of worship. We can pray, sing, play musical instruments, dance, arrange flowers, create works of art, or sit still in awe-filled silence. God delights in all expressions of worship, and our hearts also lift when we give expression to our creativity in worship. As you reflect on the wonder of creation in the form of your unborn baby, we encourage you to use whatever forms of worship are meaningful to you, and even to experiment with some you haven't tried before.

Reflection

- How do you feel about the wonder of this miracle of creation forming within you?
- How would you like to respond to God?

Encountering God as Love

If the heart is the ancient symbol for human identity and human vitality, it is also a powerful symbol for the fiery love of God.
—Flora Slosson Wuellner, *Heart of Healing, Heart of Light* [4]

About halfway through my first pregnancy, I became aware that I had fallen deeply in love with my baby. Without knowing what she would look like or be like, whether she would play soccer or prefer swimming, or hate broccoli and love carrots, I knew that I felt a passionate commitment to this baby that did not depend at all on who she would turn out to be.

About the same time, I realized that my baby had no idea what love was and certainly wasn't able yet to love me back. This did not affect my love for her. I had the incredible privilege of loving utterly and unselfishly, knowing that my love did not depend on the baby loving me in return. My love was unconditional.

Slowly the realization dawned on me that this was how God felt about me—that even before I was aware of God or knew that God existed, God loved me passionately, unconditionally, and forever. For the first time I began to understand the extent of God's gracious love for me and for all people. I had believed for a long time that accepting God's love for me was just the first step of faith, and that as I matured, God would guide me into deeper issues of spirituality. It has taken me a while to understand that love is always at the center of our spirituality. It is the key to our relationship with God and with others. Each time I have had a significant experience of God's presence, it has only reminded me in a new way that God is love.

During my second pregnancy, I felt another dimension of God's love and grace. I was in my fifteenth week when I contracted German measles. As soon as the doctors made the diagnosis, they called my husband and me to a meeting. The news was devastating. They told us that in all likelihood our baby would be blind or deaf and would have heart defects and severe brain damage. If I carried the baby to full term, it probably would not live for more than a few weeks. They knew that they could not make the decision for us, but they suggested termination of my pregnancy.

Love is always at the center of our spirituality. It is the key to our relationship with God and with others.

I entered a place of no sleep and no rest, of unrelenting questions and constant inner wrestling. Our friends and family could not offer advice; most just sat with us in helpless compassion. I did a lot of research, and everything I found painted a fairly dismal picture. I wish I could have decided instantly that no matter what was wrong with my baby, I would never consider termination, but this was not the case. My main stumbling block was I had another little one to consider.

Could I choose between these two children, one a bright, active toddler and the other unborn, unknown, possibly severely handicapped, and yet still mine? How could I reject what my whole body, mind, and spirit were working to protect? And yet, what did my responsibility to my other little girl require of me?

Then we were offered a sign of hope. After another round of tests, the doctors began to feel that this was a secondary infection and therefore our baby was probably in less danger than originally thought. We took this as the sign we were looking for to keep our baby and continue with the pregnancy. We believed this was God guiding our decision making.

After we made the decision, a peace came over me that one way or another, all would be well. I couldn't be sure that there would be nothing wrong, but I was relieved we had decided to keep the baby, and that was good enough for me at that moment. A scripture verse offered me comfort and reassurance: "He tends his flock like a shepherd: he gathers the lambs in his arms and carries them close to his heart; he gently leads those that have young" (Isa. 40:11, NIV). Even now I get emotional when I read those words that were so precious to me in those days, so real and so personal, as if God had written them just for me.

When our baby was born, she was a healthy, beautiful little girl. She is our miracle baby, and she likes to remind us of this at key moments. Her life is an incomparable gift, and so was our experience of God's care for us and both of our girls. This story will forever be embedded in my being, supporting my faith in God's gracious love, guidance, and provision.

Reflection

- How do you know God loves you?
- In what ways have you experienced God's grace and love during your pregnancy?

Encountering God as Mother

> Birthing God, be with me as I labor to bring forth what is within
> me.
>
> —Jan L. Richardson, *Sacred Journeys*[5]

In Jesus, God became personal and real to the human family. Jesus
introduced us to a God who is not distant and disapproving but who
desires intimacy and freedom in a mutual relationship of love and
commitment. He summed up this relationship in the beautiful name
he called God, Abba. *Abba* is best translated as "Daddy," a term born
out of love and familiarity. Jesus not only used this name for God,
but he also lived the relationship. He spent time alone with his daddy,
gaining strength and wisdom from his conversations with God. And
God affirmed him as his beloved Son. In fact, Jesus lived so closely
aligned with the will of his Father that he could say to Philip, "Anyone
who has seen me has seen the Father" (John 14:9, NIV).

Women may benefit from knowing that scripture contains a
number of feminine images for God, many of them portraying
God as a mother. God's mothering nature is beautifully described
in Isaiah 66:13—"As a mother comforts her child, so will I comfort
you" (NIV)—and in Hosea 11:1-4, which speaks of God leading
Ephraim, teaching him to walk and bending down to feed him. God
is even described as giving birth:

> Like a woman in childbirth,
>   I cry out, I gasp and pant.
>   —Isaiah 42:14, NIV

> You deserted the Rock, who fathered you;
>   you forgot the God who gave you birth.
>   —Deuteronomy 32:18, NIV

To describe God's longing for a broken people, Jesus employs
the image of a mother hen protecting her chicks by gathering them
under her wings (Matt. 23:37).

Scripture captures not only the gentle, comforting nature of a mother's love but also the wildly fierce and protective love that a mother can display when her children are in danger:

> Like a bear robbed of her cubs,
>   I will attack them and rip them open.
>   —Hosea 13:8, NIV

As we venture into motherhood, it can be reassuring to encounter a God who understands a woman's experience. God is described as giving birth and nurturing babies and children, as well as protecting them in the face of great danger. God is like a mother to us, loving and caring for us in this way. We can turn to God as Mother with all our worries and anxieties, joys and hopes, sharing with an open heart because God really does understand.

Ten-year-old Shah Sahman wrote this about her mother:

> There is nobody I know like my mother. My mother is like the earth, full of goodness and strong.
>
> When I'm asleep my mother lights up the dark corners and gently wakes me up.
>
> When the day comes hot and stuffy, my mother cools me like the rain does.[6]

As mothers our hearts (and eyes) can fill up at the beauty of the words she has written. But this quotation also expresses what I feel when I think of God and how God relates to me.

Kim used these images to describe her experience of God:

> I am the One who sets your heart beating
> I am the One who stills it to rest
> I am the Giver, the Gift, and the Giving
> I know all your worst and believe in your best
>
> I am the womb that holds your becoming
> I am the contraction that pushes you on
> I am the Mother who nurses and holds you
> I will be with you when all else is gone

Understanding or even beginning to describe God lies beyond both our language and our imagination. That is why scripture is rich with symbols and images of God. Pictures, similes, and metaphors are the closest we can get to describing the various aspects of God. We can encounter God as creator, provider, guide, teacher, father, mother, and even as midwife.

Both Psalm 22 and Psalm 71 speak of God as the one who brought us out of our mother's womb. God is pictured as the midwife who delivers us into our mother's arms and who can be trusted completely. It is especially wonderful for expectant mothers to have a biblical image of God as a midwife who accompanies us through our pregnancy and who will be there at the birth to support us and guide our baby into the world.

Reflection

How does thinking of God as mother or midwife affect your relationship with God?

Encountering God as Protector and Healer

> Healing (in its fullest dimension) is salvation actually taking place here and now.
>
> —Francis MacNutt, *Healing* [7]

God has put in place wonderful protective mechanisms that provide the best environment for our baby to grow strong and healthy. For example, the placenta acts a bit like a sponge, soaking up many harmful agents that may be present in a mother's blood before they are passed through to the baby. But the placenta also allows our antibodies to pass through to our babies, providing them with immunity to all those diseases that we are immune to. For me, this is truly wonderful, that our babies benefit from our life experience, even the bad times when we were ill. Nothing in our lives is wasted!

The wonder of God's protection is that we usually don't even know when we have been protected from an impending danger. How many times have you or your baby faced some potential danger only for it to be averted by a natural system or even by God's intervention? We cannot really know. All we know is that we protect our babies as much as we can through the choices we make, and for the rest we ask for God's protection and choose to trust God.

Many moms might end up questioning God's role as protector in the light of their pregnancy experiences or their baby's health.

At this point we are stepping out onto shaky ground. We realize that while God does protect our babies in many ways, some of which we are aware and some of which we are not, things can still go wrong. We all know of, and some have even lived through, challenging and often painful situations where problems have arisen during pregnancy. Many moms might end up questioning God's role as protector in the light of their pregnancy experiences or their baby's health.

There are no easy answers to why bad things happen, or why they happen to particular people, and to address these questions in any depth lies beyond the scope of this book. The bottom line is that we may never be able to answer "why," but we believe, as we have mentioned before, that "what" questions can help us connect with the strength and resources we need to handle difficult situations: What will it take for me to cope with this situation? What resources are available to me? What is the next step I have to take to keep sane, rebuild my life, find help? If God spoke to me right now, what might God say?

It is also at times when things have gone wrong that we become aware of God as healer. Healing is another complex issue, and the encounter with a God who heals is perhaps best told through Debby's story. Her story is one of sadness and suffering, but it also reveals the hope of healing and renewed faith. There are two reasons why we feel it is important to share Debby's story. First, her story acknowledges that things do not always work out as we planned or prayed. Second, this story celebrates the healing that God can bring and the hope that persists despite our struggles.

Debby's first pregnancy went smoothly, and she gave birth to a healthy girl. Debby was grateful but took her positive experience pretty much for granted, as most of us do. However, during her second pregnancy, she began to feel uneasy about the irregular pattern of her baby's kicking. An investigation showed that the baby's one kidney was enlarged. Debby was told that this condition was not serious, as the problem could be corrected surgically. This was Debby's response:

> I had a deep-seated feeling that, despite all the reassurances from the doctor, this baby wasn't going to be healthy. Perhaps God was preparing me for what lay ahead.

When Tessa was born, it soon became apparent that she couldn't suck or swallow and that she was probably blind and deaf. She was also profoundly mentally handicapped. Her minor kidney problem was insignificant now, and the doctors did not expect her to live long. Drawing on her professional training as a nurse, Debby chose to take Tessa home. At three months of age Tessa developed pneumonia and died. Debby honored the short and difficult time she and her family shared with Tessa in these words:

> We learned so much from her, and I could see God's hand on our lives.

Debby and her husband were devastated by Tessa's disabilities and death and wanted to reassure themselves that the same situation would not happen again if they chose to have another child. Eventually tests revealed that the cause of the problems was not genetic, and medical personnel assured Debby and her husband that with a carefully monitored pregnancy, the same situation was unlikely to recur. Overjoyed, they began trying for another baby. This is what Debby had to say about getting pregnant again:

> I found out just a couple of days before what would have been Tessa's first birthday. I'm convinced this was her present from heaven to her mummy, and I think God knew that if I had too much time to think about it, I might change my mind! Amidst the jubilation was a certain amount of anxiety. I was, quite frankly, terrified of having another baby like Tessa.

Unfortunately, Debby's third pregnancy was not without trauma. She fainted for the first time; blood tests got mixed up; and then the doctors discovered this baby also had an enlarged kidney, like her sister. Debby responded by praying.

> I prayed for Tarryn, for each part of her: for her spiritual well-being as well as her physical and emotional well-being. I had moments of panic and tears and have to say that God and my friends and family were very patient with me. Many people were praying for us and, I believe, carried us through that time.

God answered her prayers by reminding her of God's presence:

> Early on in my pregnancy I was showering, and this beautiful beam of light shone on my tummy just where my uterus was. It was as if God was saying, "I'm blessing this baby for you." Later on, through Bible readings, God kept reassuring me that he was indeed in control despite what was going on.
>
> A short time before the due date, there was a sermon on healing at church. I felt God was saying, "Ask for prayer for this baby's kidney." This took lots of courage, but I asked two wonderful ladies from the healing ministry at church to come and pray with us. They prayed for her kidneys, they prayed for her well-being, and I wept my way through the prayers like I was the baby!

I slowly reached the stage by the end of the pregnancy where I trusted God enough to say that even if we had another baby like Tessa, I knew God would get us through it.

This is the kind of faith and trust that only God can give.

Tarryn was born by cesarean section, and an ultrasound showed completely normal kidneys, which astounded the doctors. Tarryn is now six years old, a bright, cheerful little girl with an awareness of God that amazes her mother. Her life gives testimony to God's healing work at every level of their lives. These are Debby's last reflections after sharing her story:

> It's hard to accept that babies like Tessa are born and suffer despite all the prayers. I guess we cannot lean on our own understanding. Sometimes we have to accept that God doesn't always answer our prayers the way we expect, but he does promise that he will be with us through whatever happens in our lives.

Any discussion of God as healer raises many questions. We each have our own ideas and understandings based on what we have been taught and our own experience of God. Debby's story reminds us that healing is a complex issue, but it is one that is very close to God's heart. I believe that God's heart aches for us in our pain, and God's healing is an expression of God's immense love and compassion for us. We will look more closely at the question of healing and wholeness in the chapter "Becoming Whole." For now, let's take our questions, as well as our certainties, to God and ask God to encounter us as our protector and healer.

Reflection

- Pray for Debby and her family and their continued healing, and for all parents who have lost children.
- Reach out to someone in your community who has a child with a disability.

Encountering God as Mystery

> Pregnancy and childbirth inevitably teach us about surrendering
> to forces greater than ourselves.
>
> —Harriet Lerner, *The Mother Dance* [8]

Over the years I have had the privilege of praying with and for a
number of women who have battled to become pregnant and who
have tried various medical interventions, sometimes over several
years. These experiences have made me realize that despite all the
knowledge and scientific understanding available today, the
conception of a new human being is still a mystery. We cannot make
it happen by sheer force of will or even by intricate scientific proce-
dures. There is an unpredictability and surprise about when that
spark of life is ignited. It is the beginning of the mystery of life in all
its complexity and simplicity.

Despite several miscarriages, Corine was struck by the mystery of
conception and her sense of God's part in it each time she became
pregnant. This led her to worship in her own unique way:

> My picture of God is filled with a positive sense of awe and
> wonder and mystery. Pregnancy, to me, was also awe and wonder
> and mystery. The sheer miracle of it all definitely made me feel
> more spiritual. I am not the greatest pray-er, but with each new
> pregnancy, that basic human instinct to connect and communi-
> cate with God kicked in. With my last pregnancy, I jumped into
> my car as soon as I found out and drove to a nearby game reserve.
> As my two-year-old sat on my lap breast-feeding, I frantically
> talked to God about the rice-grain-sized life I had just discov-
> ered. A toddler, a pregnancy, the beauty of nature, and a God to
> talk to—perfect!

However, dealing with mystery is not always easy. Because
mystery cannot be controlled or explained and often seems messy
and unclear, we may respond to the mystery of God with fear or
anger. This is how Sara responded as she struggled through her
second pregnancy, battling to convince her caregivers to support

her desire to give birth naturally after previously having an emergency cesarean. At the same time she was having to deal with difficult family issues:

> To be honest, I tried to connect more with God during my pregnancies, but I found it really hard. First, I was aware that God was with me, but I didn't experience a real closeness with him that I have had in the past (and that surprised me). In retrospect, I think I was just trying to cope with all my feelings, and my husband was away for most of the pregnancy.
>
> Second, I felt angry with God because I was having to travel along a much more difficult road this second time to have my baby naturally. I felt alone, and my support networks were falling apart around me due to another family crisis, which drained everyone, including me.

Sara's story helps us realize that our encounters with God during our pregnancy may not always be joyful or uplifting. At times we may feel angry, frustrated, and sad. But what also struck me about Sara's story is that we don't need to deny or ignore our feelings—I certainly believe God doesn't. God already knows how we feel and is not intimidated or put off by those feelings. Second, despite what we may feel, as Christians we believe in a God who has promised never to abandon us. God was there at the times Sara most needed reassurance and encouragement:

> Toward the end of my pregnancy, God gave me a promise in Psalm 20:4-5: "May [God] give you the desire of your heart and make all your plans succeed. [Then] we will shout for joy when you are victorious and will lift up our banners in the name of our God. May the LORD grant all your requests" [NIV]. Well, God gave me that promise, and even though it was tough going, I did manage to have a natural birth and not have a repeat cesarean.

Perhaps when we face the mystery of God and have trouble understanding God's presence or God's apparent absence, we can pray this prayer written by Jan L. Richardson:

Divine Mystery, blessed be you in all your forms! Widen my imagination, that I may glimpse you in the hidden places. [9]

Reflection

- What has puzzled or angered you during your pregnancy?
- Tell God about how you're feeling—even if you're puzzled or angry with God.
- What do you think God says in reply?

Encountering God with Gratitude

When I was pregnant with the twins, I was enveloped with a sense of contentment, knowing that God was in control and that his grace was sufficient for me. I experienced such a sense of God's faithfulness to me, first in providing an awesome husband who supported me and prayed with me for our precious growing babies, and second by giving me an opportunity beyond all my expectations—the privilege of being a mother! I'm so thankful to God. I believe that being pregnant and experiencing the joy of having children have given me a tiny glimpse into the amazing heart of God. What a privilege!

—Eve

We may respond in many ways to our encounters with God during pregnancy. We may doubt, question, and shake our fist at all that seems unknown and unfair. We may worship and rejoice in the miracle we are living. But often all we can do in response to God's incredible gifts to us is to express our gratitude. An outpouring of thanks often arises spontaneously within us when we encounter the God who gives us life and hope, who cares for us with compassion and fierce protection, who loves us before we could imagine loving in return, who heals us in profound and unexpected ways, and yet who remains forever a mystery.

Mark's Gospel tells the story of the woman who enters Simon's home carrying an alabaster jar of expensive perfume. She breaks the jar, pouring the perfume onto Jesus' head (Mark 14:3) as an act of gratitude. We do not know what Jesus did for this woman, but his love must have touched her life deeply for her to respond so extravagantly. Expressing our gratitude to God is like pouring perfume on God's head to thank God for the amazing gifts we have been given.

Reflection

- What are you grateful for thus far in your pregnancy?
- How would you like to express your gratitude to God?

Invitation to Prayer

Through pregnancy we have been given the awesome privilege of becoming partners with God in creation—cocreators, if you like. We have also become "conurturers" to the little beings inside us. It is therefore also our privilege and responsibility to pray for the babies growing in our wombs.

I am not referring to the kind of prayer that consists of bringing our lists of worries to God. This kind of prayer has its place, and God expects us to pray through our concerns and fears, but it is not the same as actively and positively praying for our baby's well-being. If you struggle with worries and fears for your baby, take some time now to talk to God about them and to listen for God's response. When you have found a measure of peace, lay them aside and settle down to pray your hopes and dreams for your baby.

Before you pray, you may find it helpful to ask yourself some questions in order to pray with greater honesty. Consider such questions as these:

- Why do I desire this for my child?

- What effect might my desire have on my child?
- What does God desire for my child?

As you begin to pray, remember that God too wants the very best for your baby. Rest your hands gently on your abdomen, cradling your "bump." Our hands symbolize love, strength, and healing. Spend some time in silence, "holding" your baby in this way, just loving this unknown little being who has been given to you to nurture for life. Breathe gently and deeply, allowing the baby to feel your presence and contentment in this moment.

Spend some time thanking God for this precious baby. Think of the privilege of having this baby form and grow inside you. Think of the uniqueness of this new human being coming into the world. Reflect on the marvel of creation and the hope that this new life brings. Share your deep thankfulness to God for all you have received through your pregnancy.

As you begin to pray, remember that God too wants the very best for your baby.

Now express to God your deepest desires for this baby. These may range from physical health to a loving and supportive marriage partner. Pour out your wishes for this baby's life, enfolding the baby with positive thoughts for his or her growth and development into a whole and mature person.

We can also join with God in picturing the healthy development of our baby. As part of your prayer, you may wish to imagine cells multiplying, bones being knit together, organs functioning, and a little heart beating rhythmically. You may picture your baby being adequately nourished and protected through the placenta and amniotic fluid. Pray for the positioning of your baby for an easier delivery. Pray for the development of your baby's spirit, that he will be loving and kind and compassionate, open to others and especially to God. Pray for her relationship with God, that she will grow to love and serve God with all her heart, mind, soul, and strength.

Scripture offers us some beautiful prayers that we can draw on as we pray with confidence and joy for our children. One such prayer is Paul's prayer for the believers in Ephesians 3:16-19 (NIV). You can adapt the words of these verses to make the prayer more specific for your baby:

Gracious God,
I pray that out of your glorious riches you may strengthen my baby with power through your Spirit in my baby's inner being, so that Christ may dwell in his [her] heart through faith. And I pray that this baby, being rooted and established in love, may have power, together with all the saints, to grasp how wide and long and high and deep is the love of Christ, and to know this love that surpasses knowledge—that my baby may be filled to the measure of all your fullness. Amen.

What's in this chapter?

God longs to touch our wounded places with healing love and restore us to wholeness so that we may love others, including our baby, more deeply. This chapter invites us to acknowledge the wounds we carry; to receive God's gentle compassion, forgiveness, and healing; and to begin the journey toward forgiving those who have wounded us.

- Pregnancy as an invitation to wholeness
- Acknowledging our wounds
- Facing the wounds within our families
- Facing the wounds of loss and grief
- Receiving God's compassion
- Receiving God's forgiveness
- Forgiving others
- Invitation to Prayer: Praying with scripture

7

BECOMING WHOLE

The life of the spirit is never static. We're born on one level, only to find some new struggle toward wholeness gestating within. That's the sacred intent of life, of God—to move us continuously toward growth, toward recovering all that is lost and orphaned within us and restoring the divine image imprinted on our soul.

—Sue Monk Kidd, *When the Heart Waits*

Kim. . .

I vividly remember the day I entered into battle with my body. It was about halfway through the morning when all the girls in my third-grade class were summoned to a visit with the district nurse. We giggled and chattered all the way to the examination room, where we had to strip down to our panties before being examined, weighed, and measured, one by one.

The nurse looked me up and down and asked pointed questions about my eating habits. For the first time I felt ashamed of my body and wanted to hide from her gaze, although I wasn't sure why. I sensed that something must be wrong with me, and this was confirmed a few days later when my mother received a letter from the school pronouncing me "obese." The letter provided helpful details of where I could go for instruction and monitoring in order to lose the extra weight.

From that moment on it seemed that my body and I were no longer one. My body was a problem that I had to fix. By sheer strength of will I had to ignore what my body was telling me, as I could no longer trust it. Hunger was not real hunger but greed. Desire was deceptive and could not be acted upon. My mind had to plan and control my eating, because clearly my body had failed me on that count.

What followed were years of yo-yo dieting, losing and gaining weight, with every experience confirming my growing conviction that not only had my body failed me, but it was also deliberately acting against my best attempts at control and weight loss. My body became an enemy that represented all the weakness, vulnerability, and chaos within me. It had to be subdued.

Bulimia, and later anorexia, found fertile soil in my struggles with my body, and the struggles became a life-and-death battle. The turning point came when, out of sheer exhaustion, I gave up and found God waiting for me with open arms at the end of my strength. I stopped waiting for a quick and easy healing (on my terms) and turned my will to choosing life, mouthful by terrifying mouthful. However, the wounds left by the battle with my body ran deep, and my journey toward healing has been slow and often arduous.

I was about four years along on this journey when I became pregnant. My body and I had called a truce for the purposes of conception, but our conflict was far from resolved. However, from the moment I knew I was carrying a child, something shifted in my feelings toward my body. My body was no longer an enemy or a nuisance; it was the very place in which I was cooperating with God in fashioning and forming a brand-new little being. I was awed that such a miracle could have taken place and that my body made it possible. I had a new respect for a body "fearfully and wonderfully made" (Ps. 139:14, NIV).

I began to feel gratitude and compassion toward my body and deep regret for what I had subjected it to. I realized that I had to begin to pay attention to my body and respond to its needs. This process was easier because I was doing it for my baby.

The thought of gaining weight during pregnancy still frightened me, but the possibility of harming my baby was far more frightening. I made a conscious commitment to nurturing my baby through my body, which meant giving myself permission to eat when I was hungry, to rest when I was tired, and not to punish myself if I did not exercise daily.

I still struggled a lot during the first few months when I felt like I was just gaining weight. But as soon as the pounds consolidated into a neat, round belly, I actually began to like my new shape. I found my roundness extremely sensual and began to appreciate and enjoy my body in a way I never had before.

Two years later, nearing the end of my second pregnancy, I was able to embrace my body more fully as a friend and acknowledge that my body was as much me as my thoughts and feelings. I wrote this in my journal:

> I don't have to fight my body. It is holy ground. It is me. It speaks to me of what it needs. Can I befriend it and listen to it? Can I meet its needs? It is *not* the enemy. It is not involved in some subversive plot against me. I am caught up in a culture that turns me against my body and encourages me to respond to it with fear, loathing, hatred; to punish it, to control it, and to suppress all its appetites—for food, for touch, for rest, for sex, for nurture. *Why?* Who benefits? Not me. Not my body. Not my daughters. I want to nurture my body, to care for it as I would for Caydn and for our growing baby.

I could not have anticipated that the very changes that terrified me during pregnancy would become a means of grace and healing in my relationship with my body. I expected my pregnancy to be all about the baby, so it surprised me when it became a journey of growth for me as a woman, a journey toward wholeness.

Pregnancy as an Invitation to Wholeness

> Do not cling to events of the past
>> or dwell on what happened long ago.
> Watch for the new thing I am going to do.
>> It is happening already—you can see it now!
> I will make a road through the wilderness
>> and give you streams of water there.
>
> —Isaiah 43:18-19, GNT

It was quite a revelation to me during my pregnancy that God was as interested in my growth and well-being as in my baby's. But I have realized that God always desires for us to receive healing love in our wounded places, allowing us to love those around us more deeply and honestly. God reaches out to us constantly with words of life and hope, and the time of pregnancy is no exception. Perhaps there is an even greater urgency in God's invitation during this time because God knows that our own capacity to give and receive love will profoundly influence the child who has been entrusted into our care. And often during times of change or transition, we are more open to hearing and responding to the whisper of God's love.

Through the transitional time of pregnancy God invites us to release the past and embrace the fullness of the now. This does not mean that we deny or forget, just that we become open to the new things God wants to do within us. However, God's invitation may not always come to us as a pleasant experience. It may come in an unexpected and sometimes painful awareness of the hurtful dynamics of a relationship or the brokenness within our lives.

When Cary was expecting her second child, a daughter, she suddenly found that she could not bear to have her mother touch her or even be near her:

> Our relationship had never been easy, but I was completely surprised and overcome by the strength of the loathing that rose up in me. I felt I needed to protect my baby from my mother.

Cary realized that the powerful emotions she felt were not actually about the here-and-now experience of her pregnancy but were a legacy of the wounds she had suffered over many years. The feelings alerted her to the fact that her relationship with her mother was still a source of pain, and she chose to undertake a journey toward healing.

This is how Cheryl described the unexpected feelings that arose during her pregnancy:

> Carrying a baby inside of me brought with it many feelings that I had not readily accepted as part of my being. Self-doubt and lack of confidence were big for me. Could I do this? How was I going to do it? What would happen if I made a mistake? Recognizing these feelings and finding the answers through other people's experiences and relating them to my own helped to give me a different perspective.

Sara also found pregnancy to be a time when she could no longer ignore the painful stories of her life:

> I suppose at some point in your life you have to face up to all that's happened to you, and often for women that occurs when we feel the most vulnerable: while we are pregnant or at home with a baby.

Such experiences are difficult and may not be what we expected during pregnancy. Even so, we may be helped by recognizing them as God's invitation to us to journey through the pain toward wholeness.

In "Listening to Our Stories" we invited you to spend some time remembering and reflecting on your life story. Perhaps as you worked through the chapter, you encountered some wounds in your own life that need healing. These wounds may have been inflicted by people, by institutions, by systems, or, as in my story, by the very ideas our culture holds true. You may have been wounded by events beyond your control, such as loss or trauma, or by your own choices and actions.

In encountering our wounds, it can be a source of comfort and hope to know that we follow a wounded God—a God who bears the scars of a whip across his back, nails driven through his hands and feet, and a spear thrust into his side. God understands our pain. And God longs to transform that pain and restore us to wholeness.

When we approach God to seek healing for our wounds, I don't believe that we need to learn any particular techniques or formulas, recite any special prayers, or perform any elaborate rituals. We do not even have to know anything about healing. Ultimately the journey toward healing involves getting to know the Healer who works so patiently with each one of us.

> *Ultimately the journey toward healing involves getting to know the Healer who works so patiently with each one of us.*
> ❧

All we need to do is to stop distracting ourselves from our pain long enough to hear God's gentle voice of love, which is the deepest foundation of our healing. And we need to willingly take the risks of honesty and trust. We need to open ourselves to receive and respond to God's love.

This chapter is therefore an invitation into awareness—awareness of the wounds we carry and their effects on our lives. It also highlights the opportunity that pregnancy offers us to move toward greater wholeness in our lives. We can use this opportunity as we acknowledge our wounds; receive the gentle compassion, forgiveness, and healing of God; and move toward letting go of those aspects of our past that continue to cause us pain.

Reflection

- What thoughts or feelings during this pregnancy have surprised you?
- In what areas of your life do you sense God's invitation to journey toward healing and wholeness?

❧

Acknowledging Our Wounds

> Trying to build a life of spiritual disciplines on unfaced, un-healed wounds is like building high-rise structures on an earth-quake fault.
>
> —Flora Slosson Wuellner, *Prayer and Our Bodies*[1]

Who willingly acknowledges their own woundedness? Wouldn't we rather avoid pain at all costs? You may recognize yourself in Joyce Rupp's observation:

> Very few persons want to come face to face with what is painful, messy, broken, and bruised in their lives. How much easier it is to avoid what needs healing, to turn away, and to go toward legitimate forms of busyness because it is simply too overwhelming to meet our suffering head on. . . . We tend to move away from, rather than toward, what hurts us. We choose to disconnect from it rather than to approach our suffering with compassion and care.[2]

And we are rewarded for doing so, in a superficial and fleeting sense. Life provides us with many desirable options for escape when pain confronts us. We can distract ourselves with entertainment, exercise, work, alcohol, romance, medication, food, activism, sports—the list is endless. Even religion or spirituality may function as escape options. Many of us hope that our spiritual practices will anesthetize our pain and allow us to leave behind our wounds, our regrets, and all the difficult areas of our lives. We may try to use God as an easy way out.

For some of us, pregnancy itself may distract us from other areas of pain in our lives. We might have conceived a baby in order to draw ourselves and our husbands back into an intimacy we have lost. We might have sought parenthood as a distraction in our boredom, as a means of achieving status or immortality, or to soothe the ache of loneliness. And we might have been totally unaware that we were doing so.

The nine months of pregnancy also offer many distractions in the busyness of preparation. However, what I have realized is that however attractive and even noble the distractions may appear, they provide only temporary and hollow relief. Nothing changes fundamentally while I rush around, patching over the cracks, desperately trying to avoid or numb my pain. The only way to get beyond my pain seems to be to take the hard and thorny path straight through it. Only then do I open up the possibility of making peace: with God, myself, and others.

This idea is echoed by many Christian thinkers who have grappled with questions of transformation and healing. Jim Johnston gently reminds us that the way of Christian growth is not just ascent.[3] We also need to go through Gethsemane, Calvary, and the tomb before the resurrection experience. In this way growth itself can be like a birthing experience. And Henri J. M. Nouwen says:

> Do not run, but be quiet and silent. Listen attentively to your own struggle. The answer to your question is hidden in your own heart.[4]

Reflection

- How do you respond to inner pain?
- Does your usual response move you toward or away from healing and wholeness?
- How might you change the way you respond?

Facing the Wounds within Our Families

I took my new role as mother very seriously. I knew exactly how I wanted things to be: a perfect water birth, perfect bonding conditions and perfect needs-fulfillment for my growing daughter. You know the story: Where my mother had supposedly got it wrong, I was going to get it right.

—Jenna du Prees, *My Mother, My Self*[5]

The unfortunate reality of living in a broken world is that all parents are wounded and will wound their children. None of us is immune to the wounding. However, as we approach parenthood ourselves, we are offered a new opportunity to reflect on our relationships with our parents and to make peace with the tangled web of needs and expectations, fears and hopes, disappointments and dependencies that make up the relationships within our families.

Anne's was a fairly ordinary family. Her parents had three children, two girls and a baby boy. The baby was demanding, and when Anne's mom discovered five months after his birth that she was pregnant again, she was devastated. With the baby and two little girls to look after, and a husband who was often away, she felt that she would not be able to cope. She tried many different ways to end the pregnancy, but Anne is living proof that she failed. Anne says:

> My mom told me this story when I was about twelve. She also told me that she was so glad that she didn't succeed, because she doesn't know what she would have done without me.

Like Anne, many of us have experienced nurture from our parents over the years that has gone a long way toward healing wounds that they inflicted. It can be helpful to reflect on what we would like to thank our parents for, and to write down what comes to us.

We also need to acknowledge the longings that were not fulfilled, the needs that were not met, and the hurts that were inflicted. We need to tell the stories of pain and hurt that we carry with us. For many of us this can be a scary thing to do, feeling almost like a betrayal of parents who perhaps cared deeply for us and did the best that they could in their particular circumstances. We need to understand that we do this not to blame or to destroy, but to heal. As we write down our thoughts and perhaps share them with a trusted listener in the presence of God, we open ourselves to a new understanding of our experiences and the possibility of healing and forgiveness. This is evident in Anne's story as she tells of her journey toward forgiving her mom:

> I don't remember being overly worried by my mom's story, but one day while telling it to a group of people, I was horrified when I burst into tears. After a long time of journeying with a spiritual director, I came to realize that there is a little girl in me who feels that she is just not good enough. She is a sensitive and gentle little soul who needs a lot of reassurance and approval from others. The story of the attempted termination of pregnancy is there, present in the little girl.
>
> I have now taken that little girl to Jesus and let him take her hand so that he can show her a new way, a safe way, knowing that he loves her so much. She is here because he wanted her to be here, and he made her with special gifts and talents.
>
> I am now able to say the words, "Mom I forgive you," because I realize that she made decisions that seemed like the only way out for herself at the time—she didn't know me yet, or the plans that God had for me. I just trust God to show her a way to come to a place of forgiveness herself.
>
> I feel elated. I know that I have crested the top of the hill—and am facing a new dawn!

When we release our parents, we also release ourselves to begin our own parenting journey in hope and freedom rather than in reaction to our experiences of being parented. And perhaps as parents ourselves, we will gain some insight into how difficult it is to "get it right" and will extend ourselves the same grace we have offered our parents.

Reflection

- How have you responded to the wounds inflicted over the years by those closest to you?

- What do you think God might be saying to you about your relationship with your parents and other family members?

Facing the Wounds of Loss and Grief

> When it seems that our sorrow is too great to be borne, let us think of the great family of the heavy-hearted into which our grief has given us entrance, and inevitably, we will feel about us their arms, their sympathy, and their understanding.
> —Helen Keller[6]

It seems vital to acknowledge that many women reading this book have suffered loss and grief that directly affect their pregnancy. Perhaps they have lost a baby or a young child. For many women, conceiving again after losing a baby can be a strange and ambivalent experience. They may feel joy but also guilt that they are happy again. They may fear they will lose this baby as well. They may feel that some part of their life is unfinished, and they are leaving it behind in the flurry of excitement about the new baby.

Others may have lost someone close to them shortly before becoming pregnant or even during their pregnancy. Sadness can overwhelm them, and they may feel angry, afraid, and alone.

If you are having any of these feelings, may you be held in the gentle embrace of God and know God's deep compassion and presence with you through this pregnancy. There is no easy way and no right or wrong way to walk the journey of grief. Perhaps it would help you to find a companion who offers a safe place where you can share your thoughts and feelings—however strange or awful they may seem to you. And perhaps you could allow God to walk the journey with you too as a strong, comforting, and hopeful presence.

- What effect are loss and grief having on your pregnancy?
- What do you need most right now as you journey through the pain of grief? Who can you ask to meet your need?

Receiving God's Compassion

> God has so much more compassion toward our real feelings than we do. God encounters our hurting and hurtful feelings *not* as tumors to be cut out or poison gases to be suppressed, but as wounded children to be embraced and healed.
>
> —Flora Slosson Wuellner, *Prayer and Our Bodies*[7]

We spoke earlier of our human tendency to judge, deny, suppress, and turn away from our pain. In many ways we have come to believe that God responds in the same way to our weakness and humanity. However, this view of God does not seem to fit with the message of scripture or the message of the gospel.

God's compassion toward a wounded humanity reverberates through all of scripture. Scripture confronts us with reality: brokenness and chaos in the lives of ordinary people. The Bible is definitely not the place to go if you want an account of saintly perfection. The stories we encounter there are brutally honest about the good, the bad, and the ugly in all of us. The people in scripture, much like many of us, have messy, unmanageable lives that spill over the edges of respectability. Many seem to turn away from God more often than they turn toward God.

Yet, the one consistent plot throughout scripture is the story of a God who constantly seeks, calls, reaches out, forgives, and loves, in spite of the waywardness of people's lives. God is committed to humanity in ways we do not begin to comprehend. And God has compassion for all that is weak and frail within us. Hear again the words of Isaiah 42:3: "He won't brush aside the bruised and the hurt and he won't disregard the small and insignificant" (*The Message*) and Isaiah 66:13: "As a mother comforts her child, so will I comfort you" (NIV). God reaches out to us in compassion even before we turn to God.

For Christians, Jesus is the visible face of God. And in the stories of Jesus' interactions with people, we see further evidence of the extent of God's compassion and the lengths to which God will go to restore each individual to wholeness.

Do you remember the story of the sick woman who touched the hem of Jesus' cloak and was healed (Mark 5:21-34)? Jesus encounters the woman as he hurries with Jairus, a ruler in the synagogue, to the sickbed of Jairus's daughter. As they make their way through the crowds, Jesus suddenly stops and looks around, searching the faces of the people pressing up against him. A hush descends as Jesus speaks with the force of authority and compassion: "Who touched my clothes?"

The disciples find the question quite strange. Many people have touched Jesus in just the last minute—what can he mean?

But one woman knows exactly what he means. This woman has been bleeding for twelve years, bearing the physical suffering and inconvenience of her illness. But this is by no means the worst of her story. Because of her condition, the woman is considered unclean. So for the twelve years of her suffering, the woman has been excluded from her place of worship and isolated from her community.

In addition, the woman has been exploited and abused. She has visited doctor after doctor in her search for healing, and they have taken all her money without delivering the cure she so desperately seeks. Mark's Gospel emphasizes that she was getting worse instead of better. This woman had reached the end of her own resources, was isolated from family and community, and was living out her days on the margins of society.

The woman knows exactly what Jesus means when he asks who touched him. She had gathered all her remaining strength, forcing her way through the crowds so she could get close enough to Jesus to touch the edge of his cloak in the desperate hope that she would be healed. And she was. As incredible as it seems, she knows that her body was fully restored in the moment that she touched his garment.

But now she is afraid. She considers just slipping away into the crowd, but something in the gentleness of his voice, the softness of his gaze, gives her the courage she needs to stay. She falls at his feet. Her whole body trembles with fear as she bows her face so low that her forehead brushes the dust of the road.

Perhaps Jesus reaches down and takes the woman's hand, raising her to her feet. Perhaps he asks again as he gazes into her eyes with love and delight: "Who is the one who touched my clothes?" and perhaps the woman tells him her name. At his encouragement, she tells her whole story—not just the story of her illness but how it has affected her whole life, what others have done to her, how she has been treated, how she has responded—the whole awful truth. And Jesus listens. In the presence of a ruler in the synagogue that has excluded her, he listens. In the presence of the community that has marginalized her, he listens. And through his listening presence, Jesus restores far more than the woman's body. He restores her dignity and her place in society and removes her shame.

Then Jesus speaks, and his words invite the woman to begin living a new story. He calls the woman "daughter," a term of intimacy and kinship that tells her she belongs and is loved. He affirms her faith and speaks words of blessing and vocation, giving her a purpose for living: "Go in peace." Finally he restores her to wholeness in every area of her life: "Be freed from your suffering."

Jesus did not need to stop. The woman's body was healed when she touched his garment, and he could have left it at that and hurried on to the dying girl. But Jesus knew that the woman's suffering ran much deeper than physical symptoms, and he was interested in her as a whole person—interested enough to stop, interested enough to listen for as long as she needed, interested enough to set her free.

And as I read and reread the Gospel stories, I am deeply struck by the fact that Jesus dealt in a unique way with each person whose story of healing is told. Jesus had no particular formula or ritual for healing. He met each person at his or her point of need and addressed each one as an individual worthy of respect and care. And Jesus didn't heal to impress anyone or to gain fame or power. Jesus healed because he loved. Wherever Jesus was confronted with people in pain, his love and compassion went out to them, and they were healed.

The God that Jesus revealed to us has no interest in destroying or removing any part of us but longs to heal us so that we can fulfill our creative potential.[8] No experience is wasted or discarded. All can be redeemed and transformed. God makes our very brokenness whole. And we become strong again at the broken places.[9]

Reflection

Imagine that you are the woman who touched Jesus' cloak. He turns to you with a look of love and compassion, and you begin to tell him the whole story. What would that whole story be for you?

Receiving God's Forgiveness

> As a father has compassion on his children,
>   so the LORD has compassion on those who fear him;
> for he knows how we are formed,
>   he remembers that we are dust.
>
> —Psalm 103:13-14, NIV

At least some of our wounds result from our own mistakes—choices, attitudes, actions, and words that were destructive rather than life-giving. Many of us live with regret, guilt, and even shame about events in our past. Usually we try to avoid these uncomfortable feelings, but we will never find peace or move toward wholeness while running from the past. When we confront the past honestly, we can take responsibility for our actions and begin making amends. We can also begin to discern whether the guilt and shame that we feel are justified or whether we have, in fact, been the victims of abuse or manipulation.

We can begin the process by making an honest assessment of ourselves—our struggles, weaknesses, and failures—in order to recognize our need for forgiveness. The purpose of the assessment is not for us to become consumed by despair and guilt but to come to a point where we can honestly say, "I'm not perfect, and I don't need to be. But I do need to be forgiven."

Once we have made this assessment, the next step may be to write a prayer of confession to God, simply and honestly describing the ways in which we have fallen short of all that God calls us to be. It may be helpful to read the prayer aloud, to yourself or in the presence of a trusted friend, and symbolically destroy the letter. Then receive the words of grace: "Your sin has been forgiven. Go forward in peace."

Forgiving ourselves may be much harder than asking forgiveness or forgiving others. Our inner voices often refuse to let go of our mistakes and parade them before us constantly as evidence of how terrible we are. We may have trouble disputing or escaping these thoughts, but we have an ally in the gentle whisper of God.

Our journey toward forgiveness starts safely in the arms of God, where we are encircled and protected by God's love. Once we experience God's compassion and mercy, we can extend the same compassion and care to our own wounded and broken selves.

Most of us are familiar with Jesus' words in Matthew 25:40: "Whatever you did for one of the least of these brothers [and sisters] of mine, you did for me" (NIV). The King James Version uses the phrase "the least of these brethren." This scripture verse inspires us to care for others. Psychologist Carl Jung challenges us to consider how we would respond if we discovered that the least of the "brethren" of Jesus—that person who needs your love the most, the one you can help the most by loving, the one to whom your love will mean the most—what if you discovered that this least of the "brethren" of Jesus is you?[10]

Would you be willing to do for yourself what you would do for others? Could this be what Jesus meant by his command "love your neighbor as yourself" (Matt. 22:39)? Can you approach your own weakness and sin with the same understanding and mercy you would extend to someone else who is suffering?

Pema Chödrön suggests,

> It is unconditional compassion for ourselves that leads naturally to unconditional compassion for others. If we are willing to stand fully in our own shoes and never give up on ourselves, then we will be able to put ourselves in the shoes of others and never give up on them.[11]

Grasping the truth of these words is so important during your pregnancy and as you move into motherhood. It is not selfish or wrong to have compassion for yourself, to forgive yourself, to nurture yourself, to seek healing and wholeness, to ensure that you take time to rest and be replenished. Extending gentleness and compassion to yourself enables you to extend gentleness and compassion to others, including the precious baby who soon will depend completely on you to meet his or her needs.

Reflection

- What do you find difficult to forgive in yourself? What gets in the way of forgiveness?
- What might be the consequences if you do forgive yourself?

Forgiving Others

> [Forgiveness] release[s] me from the corrosive burden of anger
> and bitterness that eats away my peace of soul. . . . It also removes
> any hidden or overt effects of resentment in my way of relating to
> the other. . . . [it] affects the spirit of the person who has been
> released in ways that go beyond our comprehension.
> —Marjorie J. Thompson, "Moving Toward Forgiveness"[12]

Forgiving persons who have wounded us seems to be a vital step on our journey toward healing. To a large extent, our stories about our wounds can determine how we feel and how we choose to live our lives. When we forgive someone, we begin to tell a different story and in doing so release both ourselves and that person from the ongoing influence of the wound. We also release ourselves from the role of victim. We can then take up roles that bring life to ourselves and others.

So why do people struggle with forgiving? Experience tells us that forgiveness is by no means easy. It is true that through his words and example Jesus challenged us to forgive, but I struggle with the fact that Jesus' teachings on forgiveness have often been reduced to a simple formula that one can follow in any given situation in order to achieve peace and freedom.

In my own life, as in most people's lives, there has been much I have needed to forgive and much I have needed forgiveness for. When I reflect honestly on my own encounters with forgiveness, they were neither simple nor straightforward. No two experiences of forgiveness, giving or receiving, were the same, and the formulas simply have not worked for me. My own stories and the stories of those I have met through my work as a pastoral therapist suggest to me that forgiveness is not a one-size-fits-all Band-Aid to apply to any wound but rather a long, winding, and often arduous journey.

I will therefore avoid talking about the hows, whats, and whens of forgiveness. I just want to share three powerful images that I turn to whenever I confront the need for forgiveness in my own life.

The first image is a collage of faces representing the stories of all those persons I know who have been deeply wounded, violated, and traumatized by the actions of others. I see the face of a friend who was raped by her abusive boyfriend and then forced to marry him when she discovered she was pregnant. The collage includes the faces of family members who have been victims of violent crime, losing their peace of mind along with their belongings. In particular, I see one family who lost a husband and father in one such incident. I see the face of a friend who was rejected by a church community that once embraced and esteemed her. I see the faces of black friends who grew up under the shadow of apartheid and whose whole lives have been shaped by unjust and systematic discrimi-nation. The longer I reflect, the more faces and voices and stories come to mind.

How do you even begin to forgive, when the person or people who inflicted the pain on you do not acknowledge that they have done wrong, much less offer an apology?

I need to hear the questions their stories raise. Why should these people forgive? What would forgiveness mean for each of them? How do you even begin to forgive, when the person or people who inflicted the pain on you do not acknowledge that they have done wrong, much less offer an apology? Is it possible to forgive too soon or too freely? What is the relationship between forgiveness and justice? These are questions I cannot ignore and need to grapple with if I am going to address the challenge of forgiveness with any integrity.

The second image that I hold on to speaks to some of these questions. It is the image of the suffering Christ on the cross. This man—betrayed, condemned, beaten, disfigured, and now brutally crucified—speaks words of forgiveness to the very people who have caused his suffering: "Father, forgive them; for they do not know what they are doing" (Luke 23:34). The depth of Christ's compassion for his murderers is beyond my comprehension, but it tells me that there is no betrayal, no violation, no circumstance, and no atrocity that is beyond forgiveness.

In Christ's bleeding and broken body, he is saying: "The pain stops here. The wounding stops here. Hatred stops here. In my very body I will bear the pain of the world so that it can be healed. I will show you a different way. You no longer need to be caught up in the pattern of the world, which is to demand punishment and revenge. You can stop the cycle of hurt and violation with love and forgiveness. You can turn things around and open up possibilities for reconciliation, restoration, and peace."

This image says to me that forgiveness is neither passive nor weak. There is something very powerful about forgiveness that releases both the person I am forgiving and me from the cycle of anger and hurt. It is an active and often costly and painful choice to say: "The pain stops here. I relinquish my right to revenge."

This does not mean that justice does not need to be served. It does not mean that we accept, excuse, or condone abusive behavior or that we make ourselves vulnerable to further abuse. We acknowledge the pain and establish the boundaries we need to be safe, but we proceed in the way of love rather than the way of hatred—love for ourselves and for those who have wounded us.

In the third image that I turn to, love is what speaks to me most deeply. The image is a small reproduction I have of Rembrandt's painting *The Return of the Prodigal Son*.[13] In the painting the repentant son kneels at his father's feet. He seems to be holding on to his father's robe and resting his head against his father's belly. The father gazes down on his son with love and compassion. His hands embrace and welcome as he savors the return of this son he thought was lost. It is a powerful image of forgiveness and reconciliation.

The Rembrandt painting speaks to me of my own weakness and sin, which wound others and alienate me from God. And it reminds me of the overwhelming mercy and compassion with which

God reaches out to me time and time again. All I need to do is "[come] to [my] senses" and "set out and go back to my father" (Luke 15:17-18, NIV) to be welcomed back into God's embrace. This image says to me that only as I recognize my own brokenness and humanity and receive God's grace and forgiveness does any discussion of forgiving others even begin to make sense.

These three powerful images enter into conversation as I negotiate the path I will take on the journey of forgiveness. They challenge me time and time again to make a choice: to remain trapped in a cycle of anger, resentment, and revenge or to choose the way of love. Often the most important thing for me is simply to know that the choice is available[14] and that if I make that choice, I will not walk the path of forgiveness alone. Forgiveness is a "work between God and me,"[15] much like the growing a baby within my womb.

We may make the choice to forgive only when we realize that we can never really get even and that we will find peace only when we give up trying to get revenge. It may happen only when we become aware of how much of our thoughts, time, and energy are consumed in nursing grudges, rehashing stories, and tending to our wounds and how, in our bitterness and anger, we are becoming more and more like the enemy we despise. At a point like this we can finally say, "The pain stops here. I choose the way of love."

Reflection

- If you are on a journey of forgiveness right now, take time to reflect on how far you have come. Write your reflections in your journal.
- What is the next step you would like to take on the journey?
- What makes the journey worth the effort for you?

Invitation to Prayer

Take some time to read I Kings 17:7-16. At first glance, what do you think this passage has to do with healing?

Let's look first at the situation in which Elijah and the widow found themselves. The land was drought-stricken, the brook had dried up, and they were starving. As you look at your own life, in what areas are you experiencing drought or dryness? What areas of your life seem starved—of attention, love, gentleness, compassion, care, or forgiveness? Acknowledge those places in your past or present that feel like a desert— dry, barren, and in need of healing.

Bringing what we can is all God asks for.

Notice that in this difficult context, God sends Elijah to a poor, desperate widow. Elijah is one of God's most powerful messengers in the Old Testament, yet in his hour of need God sends him to this seemingly insignificant person, not to the rich and famous. This is important for us because it tells us that God sees us; God knows what we are going through. As small and as insignificant as we may feel and as our problems may seem, God takes note and values us still. How does this affect the way you see yourself?

Although we may feel we have nothing to give out of our poverty and brokenness, God invites us to share what we can. What the widow can give seems so meager, but this doesn't matter to God. Bringing what we can is all God asks for. In what ways do you think God is inviting you to give, to share of yourself, right now?

It is not the amount that concerns God but our faith in offering it. Even though the widow has only enough flour and oil for one last meal, she is willing to share that meal with Elijah, who is a stranger to her. This is an act of faith—when we act before we know what the outcome will be, trusting in God's mercy and goodness. What act of faith is God inviting you to take?

The result of the widow's act of faith is that her supply of flour and oil never runs out during the entire drought. We can learn some helpful lessons from this story. Although the drought did not end immediately, it did end eventually; likewise, we can trust that at some point the pain we are going through will end. Healing will take time, and there may be important lessons to learn as we travel through the desert.

But in the midst of the drought the widow had two vital resources that sustained her household: flour and oil. Flour is a basic supply that sustains us. What resources do you have that will provide the strength and sustenance you need for the journey of healing ahead? These may be such things as prayer, scripture, worship, friendship, retreats, holidays, or even a back massage!

Oil is an ancient symbol of peace and healing. This too never ran out for the widow. As you journey toward wholeness, you may recognize signs of healing, discover new insights, and experience a sense of inner growth and peace along the way. What signs do you already see that God is beginning a healing work in you?

The flour and oil served to sustain Elijah and the widow's son as well. In other words, these resources fed everyone in the widow's little community. As you draw on God's resources for your strength and healing, how could that affect the people around you? How might your journey toward wholeness enrich your relationships?

Having explored this scripture passage in more depth, what do you now think it has to do with being healed and becoming whole? Spend some time sharing with God about your journey toward healing. Perhaps you would like to hold on to these words in the months that lie ahead: "The jar of flour was not used up and the jug of oil did not run dry, in keeping with the word of the LORD spoken by Elijah" (1 Kings 17:16, NIV).

What's in this chapter?

W aiting is an inevitable and unavoidable part of pregnancy. When we embrace the waiting, we can learn valuable lessons about surrender, trust, and contentment. We can also learn to live with a deeper awareness of each present moment and to be more open to the new and unknown.

- Waiting in pregnancy
- Waiting with God's people
- Waiting in the present moment
- Waiting and resting
- Waiting in God
- Waiting and growing
- Invitation to Prayer: Entering into stillness with God

8

WAITING

Waiting patiently in expectation is the foundation of the spiritual life.

—Simone Weil, *The Simone Weil Reader*

Kim. . .

I have to be honest: I'm not very good at waiting. I find it difficult to manage the intense emotions that seem to accompany waiting—excitement, anxiety, impatience, hope, anticipation, and fear, to name just a few—so I distract myself with busyness. When I was pregnant, it was no different, and I began to read. I filled the waiting moments by reading as much as I could about the life-changing events happening within me. And my reading gave me lots of new ideas to fill the waiting time. I remember consulting list upon list of all the things I needed to buy, make, and do in preparation for my baby's birth. Then I got stuck in doing all the things a "good" mother "should" do. (Did anyone spot the myth?)

While I kept up with my usual workload, I also painted walls, bought baby clothes, and attended exercise classes for moms-to-be. I prayed for my growing baby (and felt guilty that I wasn't praying enough), sang and talked and played music to my growing bump (and felt guilty that I wasn't singing and talking and playing music enough), and prepared in all the practical ways for her coming.

However, my busyness left me exhausted. I longed for rest. I talked about my feelings with a dear friend, telling him about the pressure I felt to perform, to achieve, to get this mothering thing right—and my baby wasn't even born yet! I moaned about all my commitments, wailed over my lack of discipline, and fretted about the harm that I might be doing to my baby even then. He listened compassionately and then gently asked a question that stopped me short: "Kim, if your baby could speak to you now, what do you think she would say?"

My eyes filled with tears; the immediate response I sensed was one of love and invitation. I answered slowly. "She would say, 'Mommy, just sit down for a moment and relax with me. You don't have to speak. You don't have to sing or play classical music. You don't even have to think loving thoughts about me. Just sit and rest. Feel your body holding me. I am in you, with you. Just be with me.'"

My baby was inviting me to learn how to wait well.

Preparing for a baby's arrival provides us all with a perfect excuse for always being on the go. There are many things to be done, and we cannot avoid a certain amount of activity as we prepare for our baby's arrival. We will look at some of these practical preparations in "Preparing for What Will Be." However, our very focus on the baby who is coming may distract us from hearing God. The Leonard Cohen song "Waiting for the Miracle" reminds us of what we may be missing by focusing only on "the miracle to come."

Pregnancy is a time of waiting in which we are presented with many invitations to be busy. But it also invites us to slow down, become aware, and live more intentionally in the present moment. When we embrace the waiting, we can learn valuable lessons about surrender, trust, and contentment. We can also learn to live with greater openness to the new and unknown within ourselves, within others, within God, and within the new baby who has come to share our lives.

In this chapter we will explore various aspects of the invitation to wait through your pregnancy. We will look at our society's attitude toward waiting, what waiting means to the people of God, and what it means to wait in the present moment, to wait and rest, and to wait and grow.

Reflection

How do you usually respond to times of waiting?

Waiting in Pregnancy

> I took a course in speed waiting. Now I can wait an hour in only ten minutes.
>
> —Rod Schmidt, comedian[1]

Waiting is part of everyone's life. We wait in lines and in doctors' waiting rooms; we wait for test results and for traffic lights to change; we wait for our favorite TV program to start and for our loved ones to arrive home; we wait for celebrations and for holidays. However, in our fast-paced, technology-driven world, we are becoming less and less tolerant of having to wait. Microwave meals, digital cameras, cell phones, and Internet access all sell the promise that we will not have to wait for what we want. Our demand for instant action and instant satisfaction seems to grow daily.

In times gone by, when more people planted crops and worked the soil, people tended to live by the natural rhythms of the earth. Waiting was an inevitable, necessary, and often welcome part of life. People waited for the right season to plant and the right season to harvest. They waited in hope for rain and the warmth of springtime. They lived with an awareness of their own humanity. They knew they were powerless to direct the forces of nature and that they needed to cooperate with the created world rather than try to control it.

Pregnancy invites us into a similar awareness. Our bodies are tuned in to a natural process of growth that can neither be speeded up nor stopped. And we have no option but to wait for those landmark moments that tell us the little being within us does, in fact, exist and is growing. We wait for the results of a pregnancy test and then study our bellies, waiting for the moment when our little bump will begin to show. We wait to feel the first, faint butterfly movements. And we wait in expectation or anxiety for signs in our body that our baby is ready to leave our womb and be held in our arms.

Pregnancy ushers us into an experience of waiting that we may never have encountered before: a waiting that is unavoidable through an unfolding process that is beyond our control.

Pregnancy ushers us into an experience of waiting that we may never have encountered before: a waiting that is unavoidable through an unfolding process that is beyond our control. Because waiting is central to pregnancy, it makes sense that our attitude toward waiting can make all the difference in how we experience our pregnancy. If we accept that waiting is part of the reality and joy of being human, it may be possible for this time of waiting to become a rich resource that strengthens us and prepares us in a profound way for the challenges of motherhood.

Suzanne Mayer suggests that "for waiting to become significant and sanctifying in an individual's life, mystery and meaning, wonder and watchfulness must be woven . . . into the fabric of waiting."[2] This says to me that waiting is not about doing nothing— it is not a passive watching of the clock until "something important" happens. Waiting well is a crucial part of our preparation, allowing us to adjust ourselves physically, emotionally, intellectually, and spiritually toward a coming event. If we approach waiting with the attitude that it is to be embraced in life and especially in pregnancy, our questions will begin to change from, "How long will I have to wait?" to "How can I wait in a way that is grace-filled and life-giving?" or "How can I wait in a way that nourishes my soul?"

Reflection

- How do you feel about waiting through your pregnancy?
- Describe a time of waiting you have been through in the past that became a source of growth or nourishment.

Waiting with God's People

Waiting as a disciple of Jesus is not an empty waiting. It is a waiting with a promise in our hearts that makes already present what we are waiting for. . . .

Waiting for God is an active, alert—yes, joyful—waiting. As we wait we remember him for whom we are waiting, and as we remember him we create a community ready to welcome him when he comes.

—Henri J. M. Nouwen, *Bread for the Journey* [3]

Early on in his Gospel account, Luke (2:22-35) describes a scene that sometimes gets overlooked in its simplicity because it follows the excitement of the Christmas story. Mary and Joseph have taken Jesus to the temple to be dedicated, and they meet an old man named Simeon. Simeon takes their newborn baby in his arms and gazes at him with joy and delight. I can picture Simeon's wrinkled, age-spotted hands embracing the soft chubbiness of the baby Jesus. I also imagine Jesus looking up curiously into the smiling, weather-worn face of the old man, his cheek resting against the rough fabric of Simeon's tunic. It is a picture of contrasts—the old and the young, the wise and the innocent, one life ending and the other one just beginning.

Simeon had lived his life in hope. God had promised him that he would not die before he had seen the Messiah. So he waited patiently and faithfully until one day he felt the prompting of God's Spirit to go into the temple courts. And what was the hope that he encountered there, for which he had waited all these years? It was not a majestic king, a mighty warrior, or a charismatic leader, but instead a tiny, vulnerable baby. In the baby Jesus, Simeon recognized the fulfillment of God's promise of salvation, the hope that he had been waiting for. Now Simeon was content to die, knowing that God was faithful to all his promises.

As you journey through this time of waiting, you need to know that you are in good company. Throughout history, God's people have spent most of their time waiting. Dennis Bratcher reminds us that

> Despite what some would have us believe today, God's great acts of revelation in history do not occur every day or even frequently. . . . In fact, much, if not most, of the Bible deals with living in the long gaps between God's revelations of Himself.[4]

As we page through scripture, we encounter Abraham and Sarah waiting for the child who will fulfill God's promise to them. We see God's people enslaved in Egypt, waiting for their deliverance and then wandering and waiting for forty years in the desert before they can enter the Promised Land. We meet a persecuted and suffering nation waiting expectantly for God's promises to be fulfilled. They wait for the Messiah, who will bring justice and deliverance and usher in a new kingdom. This hope in the coming Messiah is like a golden thread weaving its way through the Old Testament.

Why did God's people have to wait for so long for God to act? I have no answer to this question but can respond only with my own conviction that waiting itself can be valuable because it allows us to acknowledge our own powerlessness. When we feel powerless, we can begin to learn to trust in a power greater than our own. The seeds of faith, hope, and trust can take root and grow in the fertile soil of waiting. The writer of Hebrews reminds us that "faith is being sure of what we hope for and certain of what we do not see" (Heb. 11:1, NIV). Whatever we wait and hope for, we need faith to believe that it will come to pass.

What strikes me as I reflect on these stories is that while the people of God waited and hoped for a different reality, they did not ignore the reality in which they found themselves. They did not sit back and do nothing. They did not sell everything and retreat to a mountaintop. They planted crops, built homes, worked, played, married, and raised families. They established communities of faith, sharing and sustaining their hope. Their waiting was active and purposeful, shaped by God's promise for the future but focused on being God's people in the present. They strove to maintain a lifestyle characterized by faithfulness and obedience to God and right relationship with the people around them.[5]

Like the people of God, all of creation has been subjected to active waiting.

Like the people of God, all of creation has been subjected to active waiting. The created world grows, thrives, evolves, and matures through time, all the while waiting in "eager expectation" (Rom. 8:19, NIV) for God to bring all things to their fulfillment. (See Romans 8:18-24.)

In waiting for the little person growing within us, we too join with all of creation in waiting patiently for "what we do not yet have" (Rom. 8:25, NIV). Allow yourself to feel your own yearnings—for your baby, for God, for all the hopes and dreams that are not yet born within you—and to stay with them for a while, knowing that you are connected in your longings with God's people through the ages as well as with the created world that sustains you. You are also connected in your waiting to a woman who waited through her pregnancy knowing that she was carrying the One who would bring life to the world, the One who would give her life even as she gave life to him.

Mary was familiar with waiting. Even before she had any idea of her sacred calling, Mary knew the meaning of "waiting well." She and her family belonged to the lowly remnant of hangers-on in Israel who still waited with hope-filled expectation for the fulfillment of God's promise of deliverance. If she had not been already firmly rooted in faith, Mary would never have understood the awesome task to which the angel called her. She could never have agreed to her holy calling if her heart had not been open and vulnerable before God and if she had not known what it meant to wait and depend on a faithful God.

When Mary accepted God's will, she allowed God to redirect the course of her life for God's own purpose. How do we respond to God, who comes to us each day in many ordinary ways, asking us to receive the life of Christ, to nurture that life, and to give that life away to those we love, to those we encounter, and to a world in need? I pray for the grace to respond to this calling with the same faith, obedience, and grateful, expectant heart as Mary did.

Reflection

- Of all the people who waited in scripture, to whom do you relate most right now? Why that particular person?
- What could you learn from his or her approach to waiting?

Waiting in the Present Moment

How do we wait for God? We wait with patience. But patience does not mean passivity. . . . It is an active waiting in which we live the present moment to the full in order to find there the signs of the One we are waiting for.

—Henri J. M. Nouwen, *Bread for the Journey* [6]

How many moments of your life have trickled away while you replayed past events over and over in your mind or planned and organized the future? If you answered "many," you are not alone. Paying attention to the present moment can often seem pointless. Our attention automatically strays back to our plans and memories, which are more comfortable and familiar, but in doing so we miss the gift of the here and now.

Why should we live in the moment? For one thing, *this moment* is all we really have. The past is gone; we can never recapture it or change it. And all our moments to come will hold their own challenges and surprises, no matter how much we plan or dream. The only moment that we have to live is now. And the only way to have any impact on how we experience tomorrow is to live our moments well today.

The present moment is also the only time when we can encounter God. Richard Rohr says that God is "hidden in full view" in the last place we look, and that is the "nakedness of now." [7] When we strip this moment of the past and the future, it feels naked and vulnerable. But in the emptiness and nothingness of now, God can meet us, fill us, and transform us.

Babies know the secret of living in the moment. For them, there is only now, and they invite us to join them in savoring it. Who can decline the invitation to stop and pay attention when the baby in your womb does a somersault that tickles your ribs or pokes a foot or an elbow into some vital organ? I can still feel the wriggling, stretching, and pushing movements of my babies in utero. I remember the joy and excitement their movements brought and how I could sit through a meeting at work, totally oblivious to the discussion, hand on my belly, in awe at the unmistakable evidence of my baby's existence.

It is encouraging to realize that, having been a baby myself, I once knew how to live fully in the present moment—and that my baby can guide and teach me as I begin to remember. My baby reminds me to experience what it feels like to be in my body right now—whether it is comfortable or not. Her rapid growth alerts me to the fact that time is fleeting and my pregnancy will soon end. So how do we live the months that lie ahead with greater awareness of now, savoring the gift of each little moment?

Recently I chatted with a friend on the phone, telling her about a particularly tough decision I needed to make. As the conversation drew to a close, my friend paused for a moment and said gently, "Kim, I wish you the strength to manage the place you are in right now." Her remark let me know she had heard me and was fully aware that my situation would not change quickly or easily. She wasn't glossing over it to some future time when all would be well; she was sitting with me in the pain and uncertainty of the present moment. We can do the same for ourselves and others, both in moments of pain and in moments of joy.

We can decide with the millions around the world who draw strength and stability from the Serenity Prayer[8] that "just for today" we will not dwell on painful memories; just for today we will not worry about tomorrow; just for today we will live in hope.

Jesus knew that we would find peace and rest only by paying attention to today. He taught us not to worry about tomorrow, for today's challenges are enough for anyone to manage. But we do not have to manage alone. In the Lord's Prayer, Jesus clearly indicated that we are to ask God each day to give us the bread we need for that day (Matt. 6:11). I believe that he was referring to more than just the bread that will sustain our bodies. We also need to ask for the bread that will feed our souls. Jesus also said, "I am the bread of life. Whoever comes to me will never be hungry" (John 6:35). Each day we need to ask for the Bread of life to fill us and satisfy us and give us the nourishment we need to live that day well.

As we begin to live our moments more fully, we suddenly become aware of the tiny treasures and the God-moments they hold, which we used to miss in our distraction. We are often surprised as we recognize and learn to "celebrate the little things,"[9] like receiving a phone call that comes just at the right time or waking from a good night's sleep. It is then possible to gather these moments into a story of life that is filled with hope and promise.

Reflection

Take a few minutes to be still. Set aside all your plans and concerns, and simply allow the experience of each moment to come to you. Be aware of what you can hear, see, smell, taste, and feel. Be aware of your thoughts, but don't dwell on them; just let them go. Afterward, pause to give thanks for the fullness and beauty of these moments.

Waiting and Resting

> Come to me, all you who are weary and burdened, and I will give you rest. Take my yoke upon you and learn from me, for I am gentle and humble in heart, and you will find rest for your souls.
> —Matthew 11:28-29, NIV

On the seventh day of creation, God rested (Gen. 2:2) and, in doing so, invited us into a divine rhythm of work and rest that is necessary for our health and well-being. Regular times of rest from our work also help keep us from becoming overly focused on achievement, which tells us we are only as good as our last accomplishment and that our value lies in what we do and what we own, rather than in who we are.

Waiting and resting were also a vital part of Jesus' lifestyle. Jesus waited thirty years before the time was right to begin his active ministry. After his baptism in the Jordan River, he withdrew to the wilderness to wait again through forty days of prayer and fasting. In the midst of his ministry of teaching and healing, he often took time to withdraw, to rest, and to wait on God. And perhaps because of this, his ministry took on a rhythm all its own.

Jesus rested at times when others panicked—think of the storm on the Sea of Galilee, when Jesus was fast asleep in a boat that the disciples were convinced was going to sink. Jesus also waited at times when people urged him to act—think of the time he waited for two days before going to visit his ill friend, Lazarus.

On the other hand, we see Jesus acting when people urged him to wait or rest—think of the Pharisees' anger when Jesus healed on the sabbath; and the disciples sending away the children at the end of a busy day, only to be rebuked by Jesus, who called the little ones back into his open arms. Jesus seemed to be guided by his own inner rhythm, the rhythm of God's plan and purpose. Unswayed by what people wanted him to do or be, he lived out his deep commitment to doing whatever his Father required of him.

What can we learn from Jesus' life as we wait through our pregnancy? Can we accept his invitation to come to him, to walk and work beside him and learn from him and thus to find rest for our souls? Is it possible for us to find that inner rhythm of hearing and obeying that helps us distinguish the important from the urgent? And can we learn to listen to our own bodies with understanding and compassion, trusting our bodies to tell us what we need, and then meet those needs as best we can?

Leigh mentioned in "Releasing the Way Things Were" how tiredness was an almost constant companion throughout her pregnancy. Like Leigh and perhaps many of you, I have never before or since experienced the same level of exhaustion as that which descended on me during the first trimester of my pregnancies. It was an exhaustion that stopped me short. I could not fight it off, although I tried very hard. Pregnancy tiredness just did not fit in with my lifestyle; it got in the way of my commitments and frustrated me intensely.

I have never found it easy to acknowledge my need for rest, and pregnancy was no exception. I felt tired throughout my first and last trimesters. Many other women seem to have similar difficulties. Gill struggled with the fact that during pregnancy, life just went on, offering her little or no opportunity for rest. But listen for another myth that gets in the way of our using the opportunities we do have for rest. It is the myth that resting is doing nothing:

> During my first pregnancy, the demands of teaching until my resignation date were heavy. Teachers tend to continue to work till the last minute, cheating on our due date, because we need the salary at that stage and because we are nervous of doing nothing and of the loneliness of being at home alone. As is perfectly normal, I felt nauseous and constantly tired, but I had to keep going. It's just as well, I suppose, as it's no good to sit around feeling sorry for yourself, but it would have been nice to have been pampered and to have had more time to rest.
>
> During my second pregnancy, I had a demanding toddler who was between fifteen and twenty-four months during this time. He certainly didn't understand that Mommy was tired and needed a rest!

I can relate to Gill's desire to be pampered. If I'm honest, I spent most of my two pregnancies waiting for someone else to give me permission to rest, hoping that someone would take charge and insist that I put my feet up, offering to meet all my commitments or reschedule my life. It happened only once.

A friend with two young children invited me to tea one morning shortly before my second daughter was born. I was glad to go, but tea and a chat were not actually what my friend had in mind. When I arrived, my friend's mom whisked my daughter off to play with the other children, and my friend directed me down the hallway into her bathroom. My puzzlement soon changed to wonder! She had prepared an enormous bubble bath, and its gentle fragrance welcomed me. Next to the bathtub my friend had placed a low table holding a stack of magazines, some freshly squeezed juice, and a chocolate chip muffin. As worship music played softly in the background, my friend left me with strict instructions to relax and enjoy.

What a luxury. I savored every minute of my bath—and the foot spa and pedicure that followed. I left her home with new energy and enthusiasm for my toddler, for my husband, and for meeting the challenges of the day.

I deeply appreciated this gift, but pampering moments seldom occur. I have since realized that I need to give myself the same kind of permission that my friend gave me, to rest and be replenished. The next step for me is to learn how to give myself a pedicure!

"But isn't that selfish . . . lazy . . . self-indulgent?" Do you ever hear these questions play over and over in your mind? I struggled with these questions for years until I came across a heart-stopping paragraph tucked away in one of the most valuable books I have ever read, *Let Your Life Speak*, by Parker J. Palmer:

> Self-care is never a selfish act—it is simply good stewardship of the only gift I have, the gift I was put on earth to offer to others. Anytime we can listen to true self and give it the care it requires, we do so not only for ourselves but for the many others whose lives we touch.[10]

I wish that every woman could write this message on her soul. You could write it on a card and tape it to your fridge, mirror, or desk. It will remind you that it's okay to give yourself the gift of rest when you are tired, the gift of solitude when you cannot be with people a moment longer, and the gift of play when life has been too serious. It also gives you permission to ask for what you need when you cannot meet those needs yourself (we talk a little more about this in "Preparing for What Will Be").

Finding the rest we need requires careful planning in our minds and on our calendars, and arranging for someone to look after our children or our other commitments during that time. We also have to discipline ourselves not to give away that time to anyone or anything else.

Reflection

- God is inviting you to be still and rest for a while. How do you respond to that invitation?

- Imagine that you are entering a room that God has prepared for you for your time of rest. What does it look like? How does it demonstrate God's intimate knowledge of you and God's care for you as a person?

Waiting in God

> In repentance and rest is your salvation,
> in quietness and trust is your strength.
> —Isaiah 30:15, NIV

Though I have often struggled with knowing how to pray, I am learning to trust that God welcomes my attempts to pray, however feeble and timid they may be. And I am learning the joy of not even trying to get it right and just resting in God. Scripture contains a beautiful invitation to rest in God that has become a shelter for me: "Be still, and know that I am God!" (Ps. 46:10).

Many times I do not even get beyond "Be still." It is all that I can do to still my body, the radio, and my own chatter and turn away from my e-mail in-box or the pile of laundry that needs doing. And so I just try to be still. When I can't even be still, then I just "be." Consciously placing myself in the light of God's love, I simply be who I am at that particular moment, the best and the worst.

Creating pockets of quiet in our lives to wait with God in prayer can be as challenging as making time to rest. Linda suggests that carving out quiet spaces requires two things: (1) a decision to make it a priority and (2) practice to figure out when, where, and how works best for us. She shares how she has created space in her life for prayer and reflection:

> I find that I can't manage a focused, quiet retreat every day. So once a week I make a note in my diary and ensure that I am free to spend some time alone in which I can focus on God, present

my petitions, reflect on how God has been present during the week, meditate on God's Word, and be still to listen to what God is saying. I've found that if I talk out loud to God, I get agitated and distracted by my own voice, so I have a journal and write letters to God and then record God's letters of reply. I am a very verbal person, so being quiet is a beneficial discipline for me.

As we journey through pregnancy, each of us can find our own rhythm and pattern of prayer that draws us closer to God on a regular basis. We are building a relationship of love, and our relationship with God will be as unique as we are. There is definitely no one "right" way, but any journey into prayer requires decision and discipline. Many people say their desire to spend time in prayer grows as they experience the depth and beauty of God's love for them and learn to trust in a God of grace. Others have discovered new dimensions to prayer during the darkest times of their lives.

Nikki was twenty-eight weeks pregnant with her second baby when she and her husband, Terry, decided to go for a 3D scan. They thought it would be fun to see what their baby would look like. During the scan Nikki noticed that the right-hand side of the baby's mouth seemed to have a line on it that looked like a cleft lip. The radiologist would not confirm or deny her suspicions, and Nikki and Terry had to wait through two long weeks for an appointment with a specialist who had better equipment and more experience.

The scan was stressful as the doctor battled to see their baby's face, but eventually the words came that Nikki had been dreading: "I'm afraid your baby does have a cleft lip as well as a cleft palate." Nikki describes her response:

> I immediately burst into tears. For the rest of the day I was in shock and cried on and off all day. I didn't want to speak to anyone. Terry handled it well, and I got angry with him for not being more emotional. In fact, I blamed him for the problem itself. I needed to blame someone. I was also very angry with God, whom we loved and served. How could he allow this to happen? I blamed God too.

During the busy weeks that followed, Nikki had trouble praying.

Although I couldn't pray very much, I knew that many other people were praying for us, and I relied on those prayers. I have often heard people say that they felt "lifted up" by other people's prayers, and that is just what I experienced.

Nikki and Terry began gathering as much information as possible, visiting the surgeon and pediatrician they would use once their baby was born, and visiting the ward where the cleft repair operations were done, so that they would feel prepared for what lay ahead. In the meantime, something beautiful and unexpected happened within Nikki:

I had the picture from the 3D scan stuck on my fridge, and I glanced at it often. As the days passed, I realized that I was grad-ually falling in love with my baby. He had such a cute little face. He looked a lot like my daughter. I began to accept that, although he was not perfect in the sense I had hoped for, he was an extra-special child and a precious gift from God.

What an experience of pure grace, that at the times when we are unable to pray ourselves, we can rest in the prayers of others. So prayer becomes a place of honesty, rest, and learning to trust in the "Love that will not let me go." [11]

Reflection

- To what rhythms and patterns of prayer are you most drawn?
- What aspects of your prayer life would you like to develop further during your pregnancy?

Waiting and Growing

> The created world itself can hardly wait for what is coming next.
> . . .
>
> All around us we observe a pregnant creation. . . . But it's not only around us; it's *within* us. The Spirit of God is arousing us within. . . . That is why waiting does not diminish us, any more than waiting diminishes a pregnant mother. We are enlarged in the waiting.
>
> —Romans 8:19. 22-25, *The Message*

Did you know that children grow far more while asleep than when awake? Their little bodies need to be at rest, muscles relaxed, breathing smooth and even, in order for growth hormones to be released. Our souls seem to work on a similar principle: in the quiet moments of waiting and rest, our souls are somehow enlarged and transformed. We cannot make ourselves grow, but we can cooperate with the process—we can provide "the time and space necessary for grace to happen." [12]

I am struck by the similarities between our experiences of "soul growth" and the experience of a baby in the womb. Your baby is growing within you in a quiet, warm place, completely surrounded by evidence of your care and provision for her, your sufficiency to meet her needs. She hears your voice faintly and probably senses your love. She can do nothing to speed up or to stop her growth process; she simply has to surrender to a force greater than herself that stimulates growth in every cell.

In the same mysterious way, we are enfolded, nurtured, and protected by God even though we may not be fully aware that what surrounds us is God. We hear God's voice faintly and sense the echoes of God's love without being able to fully understand or explain it. And all the time, God grows and shapes us through an unfolding process that is beyond our control. All we can do is surrender.

Caterpillars offer us another beautiful image of surrender to the process of transformation. There comes a point when each caterpillar somehow knows that it has grown as much as it can in its present form, so it begins to spin a cocoon around itself. The caterpillar surrenders itself to waiting and becoming. Sue Monk Kidd writes that in soul growth, "we can't bypass the cocoon. Wherever there are bright new wings, there's always the husk of waiting somewhere in the corner." [13]

Kidd shares her own story of cocooning and growth in *When the Heart Waits.* Several pivotal moments occur on her journey, and one is an encounter with a monk in the gardens of a monastery where she has gone for a day's retreat. This is how she tells the story:

> I noticed a monk, ski cap pulled over his ears, sitting perfectly still beneath a tree. There was such reverence in his silhouette, such tranquil sturdiness, that I paused to watch. He was the picture of waiting.
>
> Later I sought him out.
>
> "I saw you today sitting beneath the tree—just sitting there so still. How is it that you can wait so patiently in the moment? I can't seem to get used to the idea of doing nothing." . . .
>
> Then he took his hands and placed them on my shoulders, peered straight into my eyes and said, "I hope you'll hear what I'm about to tell you. I hope you'll hear it all the way down to your toes. When you're waiting, you're not doing nothing. You're doing the most important something there is. You're allowing your soul to grow up. If you can't be still and wait, you can't become what God created you to be." [14]

When we finally make peace with waiting, what will we discover? How will we be changed? Who will we grow to be?

Reflection
In what ways have you grown in the waiting times of your pregnancy?

Invitation to Prayer

Learning to wait as a spiritual discipline is about learning to be still and quiet in restful contentment. The psalmist offers us an image of how this feels:

> But I have stilled and quieted my soul;
>> Like a weaned child with its mother,
>> like a weaned child is my soul within me.

> —Psalm 131:2, NIV

A weaned child no longer demands sustenance from his mother like a child who is breast-feeding but has learned that as long as he is close to his mother, all his needs will be met. It is a place of dependency but not selfishness, a place of humility but also of contentment and confidence.

What does this verse mean to you? If you have ever felt something of what the psalmist describes, reflect on that time.

In this time of prayer, we invite you to enter into God's presence and to simply rest in God with a "stilled and quieted" soul. Like all disciplines, this takes practice and patience. If spending time in silence with God, with no agenda to pray either for yourself or others, is new to you, start slowly and be gentle with yourself. Begin with just a few minutes, and if you find your mind wandering or yourself getting frustrated or distracted, simply see it as an opportunity to learn and to start again.

How do we still and quiet our souls? There are many different approaches, and you may have already found a way that works for you. Perhaps the stories in this chapter have given you some ideas. We will suggest two other possibilities. Experiment on different days with each one, and see if there is one you feel comfortable with.

The first way is to use a memory. Can you think of a time when you were in a quiet place and felt a kind of trusting peace? When I was a young girl, I used to go fishing with my dad. We left while it was still dark and rowed our little wooden boat out toward the middle of the dam. Mist rose off the water's surface as the sun began to rise, the rays glinting off the ripples caused by the plop of our floats. We had to be absolutely quiet so we wouldn't frighten away the fish. It is a memory of perfect stillness and beauty.

If you have a quiet and peaceful memory, picture it in your mind now. Allow this to be the setting for your time of quiet with God. As you hold this picture in your mind, see Jesus walking toward you. Like an old, familiar friend, he sits at your side, and you share a comfortable silence together. Neither of you feels the need to say anything; you just relax in each other's company. Stay in this place until the time feels right for you to leave. Thank Jesus for spending these moments with you, and go on with your day. You may want to write down your reflections on this time and what it meant to you.

Another way of settling into a place of quiet stillness is by using our God-given senses. Take some time to use your sense of hearing. First, listen for the most distant sound you can hear, then for the sounds just outside, then the sounds you can hear inside the room, and then the sounds closest to you. Last, listen to the sounds within you: the sound of your own breathing, the sounds of the baby living inside you. As you listen, remember that Jesus breathed the Holy Spirit on his disciples, and that same breath of life is within you. God is as close to you as your own breathing. Stay with this awareness in silence until you feel it's time to move on.

Which of these prayer exercises led you most easily into a time of quiet with God? How would you like to develop this practice in the weeks and months ahead as you continue to wait and rest in God through your pregnancy?

What's in this chapter?

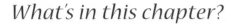

No matter how strong or independent we may feel, we need others, and this is particularly true when we are pregnant. Pregnancy can provide an opportunity to nurture and strengthen relationships with those around us and to build a life-giving community.

- Embracing our husbands
- Embracing our families
- Embracing the friendship of other women
- Embracing our other children
- Embracing our caregivers
- Receiving from others
- Invitation to Prayer: Reaching out to others through prayer

9

EMBRACING OTHERS

We cannot make it on our own, . . . we cannot become all we could be without the love, wisdom, and feedback of others.

—Larry Crabb, *Connecting*

Leigh. . .

One of the most precious memories I have of my pregnancies is lying in bed with my husband, with his head resting on my extended stomach as he waited and listened for a ripple of movement or a soft heartbeat. In this place of tender intimacy, no words needed to be spoken; we were simply together in our care for each other and for our unborn baby. This was the beginning of the strong bond we still share as a family.

As I write this chapter, I am sitting in a busy coffee shop. It's early on a Saturday morning, and I am surrounded by families and friends meeting and greeting, laughing and sharing, talking and planning, eating and simply enjoying one another's company. They are drawn here not only by the delicious aroma of coffee but by their need to spend time connecting with one another. Both in the quiet of my bedroom and in this noisy coffee shop, relationships are being built and bonds are being strengthened.

No matter how independent we may feel or how much we may take our friends, family, and community for granted, we do need others. We are probably never as aware of this as when we are pregnant. Our joy is never quite the same unless we share it with others. And in those times when we feel vulnerable and unsure, we need people to reassure us. We also need the guidance and understanding of those who know what we are going through.

An African proverb says, "It takes a village to raise a child." This proves true even when we live in busy and impersonal cities, far away from our families of origin. Children need the wisdom, caring, and attention of more than just their parents to grow into whole persons with sound values, willing and able to engage with the world around them. They thrive on attention and care received from their wider family and friends as well as from teachers, ministers, and other professionals in a variety of fields. Their relationships with these people do not begin only at birth; these relationships are being shaped even now, while we are pregnant.

Pregnancy can be an opportunity for the people who form our immediate community to pay special attention to our needs and well-being. Caroline describes it as a time of being pampered and nurtured by family and friends. In addition to providing extra care and attention, communities also may give pregnant women a special status. We may experience a new respect and acknowledgment from those around us:

> One of the positive effects of my pregnancy was the status it gave me. I got to tell the story over and over and reveled in my role as one to whom a miracle had been granted. Many people knew of the struggle that we had experienced to [become] pregnant and were very excited that the almost impossible had come to be. There was much joyful celebration with family and friends, and it delighted me to be able to share the news with them. I remember the screeches of delight, the hugs, the tears, the thanksgiving, and the laughter—the warmth of a community's acknowledgment of God's graciousness to us.
>
> —Kim

If we could choose the kind of community we want to be a part of, I wonder what it would look like. I would want it to be a place of acceptance and belonging where we offer and receive care, understanding, healing, and a listening ear. I would want to belong to a community that coaxes the best out of each person and where we find ourselves changing because we *want* to deal with sin, receive forgiveness, and become more loving.

Is such a community possible? If so, where would we find such a community? We may find it in family relationships, with good friends, in support groups or church-based ministry groups, or a combination of these.

For example, for the past nine years I have met regularly with a small group of three other women who have become eternal friends. We have prayed with and for one another. We have wept and laughed together, explored new avenues of creativity in one another's company, and listened thoughtfully to one another. These three women have been life-givers for me, breathing fresh courage, gentle healing, and renewed faith into my life.

Such communities of life seldom come into existence automatically. A group of people can build this kind of community if they will take some initiative and intentionally choose to follow life-giving principles in their relationships with one another. Perhaps God is inviting you to take the risk of establishing and helping build such a small community, or simply to take the step of joining and participating in this kind of group. If this seems difficult, consider asking God to give you what you need in the way of courage, ideas, or an opening.

Reflection

- What communities do you find yourself in at the moment?
- How could you help create a "community of life"?

Embracing Our Husbands

> Fathers, like mothers, are not born. Men grow into fathers and fathering is a very important stage in their development.
>
> —David Gottesman, American businessman[1]

For many of us, one of the most joyful experiences of pregnancy is sharing with our husbands the news that we are expecting a baby. This was true for Gill, who is grateful that her pregnancy was something both she and her husband wanted and looked forward to doing together. It is a sheer delight when our journey toward parenthood begins with a shared desire, shared love, and shared joy.

As the journey progresses, we move from being a couple to discovering a new identity as a family. This sense of "becoming a family unit, rather than just a couple" was one of the most positive aspects of Janine's pregnancy. Other women had this to say:

> During my first pregnancy I guess my relationship with my husband expanded to include the little person inside me. We both viewed parenthood as a wonderful adventure.
>
> —Debby

> My relationship with my husband very quickly and naturally progressed into "family mode." It was great to share our hopes and fears on every level and be involved in the journey together.
>
> —Corine

As much as we share in the delight of becoming a family, we also begin to sense that our relationship with our husband will change. New dimensions will be added, and we may have to let go of certain aspects of the relationship, such as the intimacy or spontaneity of just being two. You may have already experienced your "bulge" or your own preoccupations about the baby getting in the way.

With all the attention focused on the mother-to-be and the baby during pregnancy, some husbands end up feeling sidelined. Adrian, an expectant dad, commented that he felt excluded while everyone fussed over his wife, Jo—almost as if he had had nothing to do with the pregnancy! He wryly stated, "This began to seem like artificial insemination. I had served my purpose."[2] He felt ignored and resentful, then angry with himself for feeling this way.

We may have to make a conscious effort to include our husbands in our pregnancy and in our baby's development. The reality of pregnancy is something we as women experience from the inside—we cannot escape it—whereas our husbands do not have the same constant reminder. They may want to share in our pregnancy, but there is a natural distance between our involvement in the process and theirs.

At times these differences in how we experience the pregnancy can become a source of conflict. Conflict in the relationship can also arise from different expectations. I might have a very clear idea about what my husband should say and do as my helpmate during pregnancy. However, he does not have a hot wire to my brain and, in fact, he may be wired entirely differently.

Any marriage involves the joining of two very different life stories. Each of our stories encompasses different life experiences, different family values, and, sometimes, different cultural backgrounds. Our stories about the way the world works (according to our family) and the way things should be done (according to the value systems we have come to hold) can vary greatly. We may already have worked through some of these differences in our marriage, but new differences may surface when we face the task of parenting together.

Breast-feeding became an issue for Adrian and Jo before their baby was even born.[3] Jo wanted to breast-feed on demand, anywhere, at any time. Adrian felt that breast-feeding in public was exhibitionist and might embarrass outsiders. They talked this through and reached a compromise before it became an oversized issue.

We can learn important lessons from the way Adrian and Jo dealt with this conflict. First, they acknowledged the issue and talked honestly about their feelings. They also respected each other's point of view. Then they were humble enough to accept a compromise that would work for both of them, rather than insist that one way was the only way.

Acknowledging their true feelings may be the most difficult step in the process for both men and women. Like women, men are subjected to various myths about how they should and should not feel and behave as fathers-to-be. They may feel trapped by the belief that they should always be strong and shoulder the burden of new responsibilities. And they may hold back from sharing their feelings because of the myths about what men "should" feel and how they should—or should not—express emotion.

This does not mean that fathers-to-be are not plagued by fears, concerns, and doubts, just as we are. Sara's relationship with her husband was affected badly by her husband's fears. She says:

> My husband was quite negative about the pregnancy, and be-coming a father really scared him. He expressed these fears in a very negative way to me, which made me feel distant from him. I could not openly share my fears with him because he was so fearful himself.
>
> I therefore felt very alone in the pregnancy. I was worried that when the baby came, my husband would just leave, and I'd be left a single mom!

Encouraging our husbands to talk honestly to other fathers can help. We may also help them by listening to whatever they do share with us without criticizing or trying to set them straight. Our husbands are on a journey toward fatherhood just as we are on a journey toward motherhood. We may desperately want them to be a particular kind of father, just as we want to be a particular kind of mother, but perhaps we can begin to extend to our husbands the same kind of grace and compassion we are learning to offer ourselves.

Our relationship with our husband is one of the deepest connections we are called to make. We are called not only to accept each other but also to delight in each other. Often through our marriage relationship God teaches us the meaning of passionate and sacrificial love. I have been married for nineteen years, and I am still learning about the value of my husband's differing views. They balance my perspective, open up new possibilities, and add a fuller dimension to our combined efforts to live together and parent together. When we choose to listen to each other with respect and care through all the changes that we face on our journey together as parents-to-be, we make it possible for our pregnancy to become a time of growth and healing for us as a couple.

Reflection

What qualities of your husband complement your qualities and create a balance in your relationship?

Embracing Our Families

[God's] mercy extends to those who fear him, from generation to generation.

—Luke 1:50, NIV

In your pre-pregnancy days, how often did you hear the question, "Well, you have been married for _____ now [anything from five minutes to five years]. When are you going to settle down and start a family?" Have you ever really thought about that question? Do we, in fact, as individuals, "start" families? This is a distinctly Western understanding of family, where each family member is seen as standing alone, independent of the rest of the family. In most cultures around the world, people would say that they are born into families and stay in them until death—or beyond.[4] But whether your family leans toward independence or interdependence, there is no doubt that our families can play an important role in how we journey through pregnancy and into motherhood.

In earlier chapters we have done some of the work involved in reflecting on our past and the relationships that have shaped our stories. Our parents and caregivers, grandparents and elders have each influenced us in various ways. Writing especially about mothers and grandmothers, Jan L. Richardson says:

> From generation to generation our lives connect, and the lives of our grandmothers and mothers give shape to our own songs of joy, of lament, of praise, and of pain. Often the threads of our relationships are tangled, and the process of weaving meaning from them may be fraught with anger and loss. Yet by their presence or their absence, their tender care or their failures, our foremothers influence who we are.[5]

My mother has played a deeply significant role in my life. However, when I was growing up, I was convinced that once I became an adult, I would no longer need her. I couldn't have been more mistaken. I found that I needed advice and someone to talk to, someone who had experience and the wisdom of years but who also knew me intimately. I could ask my mother the silliest questions and not be embarrassed. As independent as I wanted to be and as much as I wanted to prove myself, I still needed help. My need intensified when I embarked upon the adventure of pregnancy and motherhood.

Although in every other respect we may be mature and competent, holding our own in our places of work, our places of worship, and our social circles, in relation to our mothers we are often a complex mix of needy child, rebellious teenager, independent woman, and trainee mother. Our mothers have their own mix of feelings as they face the challenges of growing older, learning what it means to be a grandmother, and wanting to be involved but not wanting to step on toes. This can lead to strained communication and even open conflict and misunderstandings. Or it can lead to delightful encounters and a renewed bond as we face a new chapter in our relationship with our mothers.

Corine shares how her relationship with her mother was affected by their journeying together through her pregnancy:

One of the greatest gifts of my pregnancies was sharing them with my mother, who was very involved and incredibly supportive. She listened to all my stories and discoveries, went with me for checkups when my husband could not make it, and held my hand through both labors. Our relationship changed because of all the sharing—and especially because she never felt threatened by my exploring ways different from her own. Her open-mindedness and acceptance made a huge difference, and I admired and appreciated the fact that she really let me be me!

Marje's experience was different. She grew up in a very conservative religious home. In this environment it was unacceptable for Marje's mother to share her own experiences of pregnancy and childbirth with her daughter. Marje says,

> I wish my mother had told me more about pregnancy. Mothers didn't inform you very much about babies and pregnancy when I was growing up.

Our mother may not be the one who becomes the reassuring guide and companion through our pregnancy; instead that person may be our grandmother. This was Esther's experience. Esther became pregnant when she was young and single. Her mother struggled to accept this and felt angry and disappointed with Esther, making it difficult for Esther to draw close to her. However, Esther found her needs for care and understanding fulfilled through her grandmother. She says:

> My relationship with my grandmother strengthened, and she gave me support and made me see the other side of pregnancy as being God's will. We had such precious moments together, and this is where my understanding of God and Christianity started. Through my granny's support I learned that the only person available to me whenever I needed him was God.

Fortunately when Esther's baby was born, her parents relented and fell in love with their first grandson, who looked so much like his grandfather!

We should not forget the role our fathers and grandfathers can play in supporting us. Many fathers and daughters have a special bond that can strengthen as they share the experience of pregnancy. You are fortunate if you share this kind of relationship with your father.

Fathers and grandfathers of a certain age may not have been present or involved in their own children's births, so they may not know how to relate to you during your pregnancy. They may want to be more involved but feel unsure about how to take the necessary steps. This can lead to an awkwardness in your relationship. Fortunately, pregnancy once again offers us an opportunity to make some changes and develop new ways of relating to our fathers—not as "Daddy's little girl" anymore but as mature women with a child growing inside us that we can be proud of and take delight in together.

In fact, for many families the news of a pregnancy is good reason to celebrate. With each pregnancy we anticipate the addition of a new member to our wider family, who will want to participate in welcoming the newcomer. Gill shares her experience of her wider family during her pregnancy:

> I didn't feel alone, as we had supportive extended families. It was not just my "own thing." There was a sense of family anticipation and involvement. My first baby was going to be the first grandchild on both sides, so everyone was very supportive and excited.

In this context, family does not mean just the family we grew up with but also our husband's family. Integrating the traditions, ideas, and backgrounds of two family systems presents a challenge. But our differences can bring tremendous strength and richness. We can create a diverse, multigifted community.

However, it may not be possible to be surrounded by supportive family members, not because they are unwilling but simply because they are not there. Shirley was living far from her family in a foreign country when she got pregnant. Her new friends had ideas and superstitions she could not relate to, and she missed the familiarity and concern of her own family. More and more families are spreading themselves around our global village, and Shirley's experience, although painful, is not unusual. There are no easy solutions to the pain of longing for those we love most and know best. It can help, though, to acknowledge the pain, express our gratitude for the family we have, try to build solid relationships in our new place, and learn to rely more on the companionship of God.

Reflection

- How do you feel about your wider family playing a role in your baby's life?
- What action would you like to take as a result of your feelings?
- If you are happy to do so, how can you involve your family in welcoming the newest addition into the family community?

Embracing the Friendship of Other Women

> When we are in a relationship that is real, open, and unconditional, we can sense the presence of God.
> —Robert J. Wicks, *Touching the Holy* [6]

Pregnancy is a uniquely female experience. When we are going through this experience, we may feel the need to connect with other women who have "been there, done that, got the oversized T-shirt." We might also seek out friendships with other expectant moms. Sharing common experiences, concerns, and practical advice can be helpful and reassuring. These relationships can offer us a sense of strength and belonging that spills over into other areas of our lives.

However, many of us are reluctant to engage too deeply with groups of women, having been hurt in the past by gossip, cattiness, and a spirit of competition rather than solidarity. It doesn't have to be like this, though. Jesus' life and teachings invite us to find a different way. His mother and her cousin demonstrate how to live out that different way through pregnancy.

We have already mentioned the special friendship Mary and Elizabeth shared during their pregnancies. When Mary arrives at her cousin's home, Elizabeth's first words to Mary are: "Blessed are you among women, and blessed is the child you will bear!" (Luke 1:42, NIV). There is no jealousy, no comparison, and no judgment from Elizabeth. She extends words of kindness and blessing to Mary and delights in her presence and the wonderful gift she will bear. Elizabeth offers Mary unconditional acceptance and an unselfish sharing in her joy. This is the kind of friendship we all would treasure and can learn to give to others.

Corine explains how she felt in the company of other women during her pregnancy:

> I felt more drawn to other pregnant women or those who already had children. I enjoyed talking about our experiences and thoughts and opinions. However, it was sometimes difficult not to be judgmental (or feel judged!) when views and ideas about pregnancy and birth differed. I tried very hard not to get into the competitive mode that seems to creep in at times: "How many pounds have you gained?" "When are you stopping work?" At times I had to really focus on the fact that my experience was personal and right for me, and that I had to respect that others had their rights too!

Caroline put it this way:

> I particularly craved the friendship of other pregnant women (I didn't know many). In some ways they are the only ones who really understand what you are going through. I also wanted the friendship of like-minded women, as this is a confusing time when all your preconceived notions suddenly have to become practical. I was grateful to have the friendship of one such woman.

In pregnancy, as in life, we will connect with some people better than others. We cannot assume that the common experience of pregnancy will ensure a lasting and meaningful friendship. However, when we find one or two special companions at this particular time in our lives, it can be a very valuable gift. The friends I made in my prenatal class were a great support through my pregnancy and my children's early years. We continued meeting through our babies' feeding and teething difficulties, to first birthday parties and potty training.

One difficulty we may face during pregnancy is a change in our relationships with married women who are struggling to conceive, or with our single friends. Corine shares her experience:

> My closest friend since childhood days had been battling to get pregnant for seven years when my husband and I got pregnant as soon as we tried. It was hard for all of us. She felt angry and jealous, and I felt guilty and uncomfortable. It was hard to pick up the phone and tell her. The gift here was our being able to be honest about our feelings and to talk through them and not feel ashamed of ourselves. This honesty brought us closer. The cherry on the top was her becoming pregnant a few months after me and our children being friends now. Like a movie scene!

The key seems to be honest communication.

Our single friends may feel that they will be sidelined and forgotten in the midst of our intense focus on our babies. This may happen in the short term. However, all friendships require ongoing effort. In our busy lives, finding time to meet with and talk to friends is always a challenge. It will remain so whether you are married, have children, or are single. If a friendship is important enough, it will survive and even flourish amid the challenges and changes that children bring.

Reflection

What friendships do you want to nurture particularly through your pregnancy and beyond?

Embracing Our Other Children

> Jesus believes and His whole message presupposes that the human heart has infinite capacities for life and love.
> —Ronald Rolheiser, *The Restless Heart* [7]

After a friend of mine became pregnant with her second child, she felt anxious that she wasn't experiencing the same feelings of excitement and awe as during her first pregnancy. Between work and looking after an active preschooler, she simply did not have the same time or energy to dwell on the precious meaning of this baby. She wondered if this also meant she wouldn't love the new baby as much as her first child. It seemed to her that the second baby was losing out and that, in some way, second meant second best.

I think many moms feel like this to a lesser or greater extent. When we are pregnant the second time or even third or fourth, we wonder if we could possibly relive the same thrill of our first pregnancy. If not, does this mean we will love this new baby less, or will the new baby be affected by our reduced excitement? Of course, it can work the other way as well. Esther's first pregnancy was traumatic because she was young and single. Her second pregnancy was pure delight because she was married, and she and her husband both wanted this new baby. They anticipated that the baby would add a welcome dimension to their family life.

One truth we can hold on to is that every pregnancy is distinctive. First, the baby in your womb differs from any baby you have carried before; he or she is a unique human being with particular predispositions and genetic makeup. This baby may move or grow differently from previous children or may affect your body in another way.

Second, you also have changed—you aren't the same person who carried your first baby. Your relationships, values, and priorities probably have changed. In the light of this, there seems to be little value in comparing the minute details of our pregnancies.

Another important truth is that the differences in our experiences of pregnancy do not mean that we have any less capacity to love a new baby. Love is incredibly elastic. Its dimensions go on forever. The writer of Ephesians tries, as much as language will allow, to describe the vastness of God's love:

> I pray that you, being rooted and established in love, may have power, together with all the saints, to grasp how wide and long and high and deep is the love of Christ, and to know this love that surpasses knowledge—that you may be filled to the measure of all the fullness of God.
>
> —Ephesians 3:17-19, NIV

Although our own love is not as wide and long and high and deep as God's, we have God's love as an unlimited resource to draw from. Our hearts, made in God's image, are designed to love and to grow in love. A new baby offers an opportunity to extend that love to another precious human being.

If we are concerned about how our older children will react to this new baby entering their lives, we need to remember that the birth order of each child in the family has pros and cons. Our first child has the benefits of our undivided attention for the first part of his life. However, he is also our guinea pig. We are usually more uncertain and worried about getting it "right" with our firstborn and may expect more from him as well. Subsequent children never get quite as much focused attention, but they profit from our experience and our more relaxed attitude. They have the added benefit of the companionship of an older brother or sister. And we can't underestimate the benefits for our older child of the challenges and joys that go along with having a younger sibling.

In addition to the emotional responses we may experience with our second pregnancy, there are various practical considerations. I battled with questions like: How soon can I potty train my toddler? When do I move her into a bed? How do I handle jealousy? What if my toddler needs me and I'm breast-feeding?

It helped me to think about these things and put certain plans into action. It was also important for me to accept that I could not anticipate everything. I had to trust that I had sufficient resources to manage the challenges that would arise. Just as God gave the Israelites manna in the desert, God give us more than enough to meet our needs, but we cannot store reserves. We have to keep trusting God for tomorrow's supply.

We also need to trust God to supply our older children's needs as they wait with us for the birth of their younger sibling. Our ever-extending tummy and all the effects that go with it can mean that we are not as available to our other children as we would like. Debby put it this way:

> During the second pregnancy I obviously had another child to care for, and so my daughter had to put up with a mommy who'd dash off to the toilet to be sick at inopportune moments and who'd flake out and not be very energetic.

Pregnancy is a time of preparation for our children as much as it is for us.

However, Debby also describes her daughter's excited anticipation of the new baby:

> We shared together the delight of the baby growing and would look at pictures of how big the baby was at different stages, and she would feel the baby move with great fascination.

We get to wonder at the miracle of life all over again through the eyes of our other children! We also have the opportunity to nurture our intimacy with our children as we share the joy of this new baby's development and birth into our family circle.

Reflection

How would you like to prepare your other child or children for the new sibling?

Embracing Our Caregivers

> Throughout history it has been a paradox that the midwife is both important and insignificant. Shiphrah and Puah, sought out by Pharoah, literally held the future [of Israel] in their hands.
> —Margaret Guenther, *Holy Listening* [8]

Shiphrah and Puah saved the Israelite nation, yet they are seldom remembered or honored. Shiphrah and Puah were the midwives that Pharoah commanded to kill all male children born to Israelite women in Egypt. They chose to disobey the order, and when Pharoah realized that many baby boys were surviving, he challenged them. They replied that the Israelite women were too "vigorous" and delivered before they could get there to help them. Their courage and crafty intelligence saved God's chosen people (Exod. 1:15-21).

We cannot underestimate the vital role that our caregivers, teachers, and birth assistants play in helping us deliver healthy babies. In Western societies we usually have many choices as to whom we would like to accompany us through our pregnancy and how we wish to deliver. There are prenatal exercise coaches and lecturers. We can consult nurses, midwives, general practitioners, and obstetricians. We can deliver at home or at a hospital, choose to give birth in a homelike setting with hospital backup, have a water birth, or choose an elective epidural or a cesarean.

When we think about whom we would like to accompany and guide us through our pregnancy and the birth of our baby, I think we would all like people who are considerate and respectful. Finding people who match what we are looking for, however, is not always easy. This was Caroline's experience:

When I was expecting twins, my general practitioner sent me to a gynecologist. After a couple of visits, I knew that I didn't like the gynecologist—he told me he would automatically do a cesarean section for twins and left me feeling as though he was in control and not me. So halfway through my pregnancy I had to find another gynecologist—a difficult decision, but it turned out to be a positive move. I found a woman, and I was much happier with her.

Just as God brought Shiphrah and Puah into the lives of the Israelite women, so God will bring just the right helpers into your life. We can pray for the help of people we can trust and feel comfortable with during this vulnerable, intimate, and ultimately holy experience.

But we will have to play our own part in seeking them out. We can do some research, ask other women whom they found helpful, and visit some of the people ourselves. God will guide our decisions as we listen to our own gut responses and discover an inner peace.

Reflection

- What qualities have you looked for as you choose helpers to support you through pregnancy and birth?
- How peaceful do you feel with the choices you have made?

Receiving from Others

We fail to receive what [God] has for us because we fail to ask. The same is true of our human relationships. We frequently are robbed of richness and closeness because we do not ask.
                    —William Backus, *Telling Each Other the Truth* [9]

In this chapter we have explored the importance of nurturing our relationships with various people during our pregnancy: our husbands, our families, our friends, our other children, and our pregnancy and birth caregivers. This can require initiative, courage, compassion, and persistence on our part. But all relationships are about "give and take," and it is important for us also to learn how to ask for the kind of care and support we need.

One of my problems, and you may be able to identify, is that I often fume silently over how much I am giving, while the other person seems to totally ignore my needs. Then when I confront the person, he or she says the same thing about me. Confusion reigns! Somehow we both are giving, but neither is receiving.

If we are going to embrace others during our pregnancy and learn to receive and return their love, we need to begin to ask clearly for what we need.

I have assumed that I know what the other person wants, and that person has done the same, and we both have gotten it wrong. Neither of us is receiving what we need because we haven't told each other what we need. We assume that if the other person really cared, he would automatically know what we needed and would give it to us without our having to ask. This unrealistic thinking places a heavy burden of expectation on our relationships that will inevitably lead to conflict.

If we are going to embrace others during our pregnancy and learn to receive and return their love, we need to begin to ask clearly for what we need. This is not as simple as it sounds. Many of us grew up in families and cultures in which it is considered impolite to ask for what you want. You usually have to wait until it is offered. Christian culture has also encouraged the attitude that asking is self-centered, and that it is better to serve and give than to ask and receive.

However, Jesus teaches us something completely different. In his Sermon on the Mount, he says, "Ask and it will be given to you" (Matt. 7:7, NIV). And when one of the disciples asks Jesus to teach them to pray, he gives them the words of a prayer in which the central phrase is "Give us!" Jesus himself responded to people's requests by healing, visiting people's homes, answering questions, and feeding hungry people. There are even times when his initial resistance to a request is overcome by faith and persistence: think of Mary asking him to avert an embarrassing situation for the bridegroom when the wine ran out at the wedding in Cana (John 2:1-11), or of the Canaanite woman who begged Jesus to heal her demon-possessed daughter (Matt. 15:21-28).

Asking is a spiritual exercise that begins with identifying and respecting what we want and need. Jesus understands this. His immediate question to blind Bartimaeus is, "What do you want me to do for you?" (Mark 10:51). What an important question! What do you want Jesus to do for you? What do you want from life more than anything else? What do you need from your relationships? What do you need right now?

This is not to say that everything we desire is good and holy. But when we bring our desires to God in prayer, the Holy Spirit helps us recognize what is motivated by selfishness and pettiness rather than by our own inner call and needs. We can then begin to ask God and others with confidence for what we need.

It may help you to make a list of everything you feel you need or want right now. Don't censor or judge your list. Even if what you write seems ridiculous, impossible, or selfish, God will help you sort it out. Too often we prevent ourselves from receiving the very things that would bring us joy and peace because we think we aren't allowed to want them.

Prioritize those five or six items on your list that seem most important right now. Then ask yourself the following questions: Which of these can I do for myself? What has prevented me from doing this for myself before? How can I overcome the obstacles? How can I make a plan to do these things?

Now, is there anything you can ask someone else to do for you? How could you make your request kindly and politely but with a gentle insistence? Perhaps you could also ask God to prepare this person to be receptive to your request and to work in your spirit and mind so you will find the best time and words to ask for what you want. Remember, however, that God does not control our free will, and when we make a request, we give the other person the freedom to say no. If this happens, try to negotiate what is possible, rather than just accepting the "no" immediately. Check what your inner, God-guided spirit is saying, but don't give up too easily!

Last, is there anything that only God can do for you? You don't have to persuade God; God already knows what is in our hearts, but because we are in relationship and because God respects our free will, God likes to be asked. Asking is also necessary for our faith to grow.

We ask God and those around us to meet our needs, not because we are demanding but because being in relationship is about giving and receiving. We are always in a better position to give when we know what the other person wants, so we not only ask for what we need, but we also ask the other person what he or she needs and try to respond appropriately. Of course, we will never meet all of one another's needs perfectly, which is why we need a community around us and not just one person. But when we are open to listening and sharing, giving and receiving, relationships seem to thrive and flourish. What better way to embrace others, especially during this time of pregnancy, when there are so many exciting things to celebrate and enjoy?

Reflection

- What do you need most right now?
- Who can give it to you?
- How can you go about asking for what you need?

Invitation to Prayer

Turn to a oft-quoted scripture passage to guide you through this prayer time: 1 Corinthians 13. But first, take time to still and quiet your heart in God's presence, using the approach you found most helpful from the previous "Invitation to Prayer." Open yourself to hearing and receiving God's gentle whisper of love. Then read through 1 Corinthians 13:1-7. Read through these verses slowly several times, perhaps even aloud.

Which words or phrases stand out for you? Why do you think these particular words hold meaning for you right now? Underline them in your Bible if you like. Make a note in your journal of any thoughts about love that come to you.

How do those around you demonstrate different aspects of love at the moment? What aspects of love do you show others?

Ask God to guide you as you think about how you could apply these characteristics of love to the various people in your life. Think about your husband, parents, parents-in-law, siblings, grandparents, friends, work colleagues, children—all the people who hold a special place in your life. What is love saying to you about each of these people? How could you respond lovingly to each of them?

First Corinthians 13 (vv. 4-6, NIV) lists several things love is not or does not do:

> It does not envy.
> It does not boast.
> It is not proud.
> It is not rude.
> It is not self-seeking.
> It is not easily angered.
> It keeps no record of wrongs.
> It does not delight in evil.

To which of these traits or habits are you prone? Spend time confessing to God any unloving things you have thought, said, or done in the past few weeks. There may be reasons for the way you reacted or behaved, and God sees those. However, God always calls us to choose the way of love. As you confess, therefore, also ask God to give you the strength, determination, and wisdom to know how to be more loving day by day.

First Corinthians 13 (vv. 4, 6–7, NIV) also lists a number of things that love is and does:

It is patient.

It is kind.

It rejoices in the truth.

It always protects.

It always trusts.

It always hopes.

It always perseveres.

Which of these characteristics come naturally to you? Which of them do you have to work on? How do you see yourself doing that? Ask God for the grace and humility to develop your ways of loving so that those around you feel your love.

Now that you have spent time in prayerful reflection, consider how you can apply your insights to your life. What specific actions— ways of demonstrating love to others—came to you in your time of prayer? Perhaps you thought of writing a letter of affirmation, making a small gift, cooking a special meal, or even taking the car in for maintenance! You may also set aside time to speak with one or two people and ask them what they need and how you can demonstrate your love for them in a way they will recognize and appreciate. Plan carefully and realistically how you will carry out these acts of love.

After you have done the things that came to you during prayer, spend time reflecting on how people responded to your actions. What have you learned about love from this experience? What is the next step you sense God asking you to take? Record your thoughts and feelings in your journal, and offer them to God.

What's in this chapter?

During pregnancy we prepare for the coming of our baby, but being prepared and getting ready mean different things to different people. In this chapter we focus on preparing ourselves emotionally, spiritually, and in practical ways to receive our baby through the process of birth and to welcome him or her into our hearts, lives, and homes.

- Preparing with God
- Preparing to welcome our baby
- Preparing our home
- Preparing for our baby's birth
- Preparing with ritual and celebration
- Preparing a name
- Preparing in faith
- Invitation to Prayer: Prayer Walk

10

PREPARING FOR WHAT WILL BE

I always take abroad with me one really good soft pillow—to
me it makes all the difference between comfort and misery.

—Agatha Christie

Linda...

Early in my pregnancy, I spent time on an olive farm in Tulbagh, down in the Western Cape of South Africa, and was awakened one night by a fire alarm. On the horizon, a band of fire approached the farmlands, and all available hands tried to prevent the groves and farmhouse from being consumed should the winds change.

We had to pack quickly. I had packed my suitcase for vacation, so I didn't have to make major decisions about its contents. What I took hardly mattered—the safety of my baby and me was far more important. But for those who lived on the farm, the choices were huge. Each person had one suitcase and a couple of hours to decide what to take. I was struck by what people chose—things like photo albums, books, a special item of clothing, and so on. Grateful not to have to make these choices, I realized that people have different ideas about what is essential and what they need in order to feel prepared.

How do you pack a suitcase? You might ask yourself questions that focus your attention on your destination and what you will need when you get there: Where am I going? What will I do there? What will the weather be like? How long will I be there? If you have any extra space, you might think about including some nonessentials and luxuries. Whatever you pack will depend on your ideas and decisions about what is essential. I doubt that any two people would pack exactly the same items for a vacation at the same destination.

Preparing for the coming of a baby is a bit like packing a suitcase. We go through a process of anticipating, planning, and finally deciding what we need so that we feel ready for the baby's arrival. Our "packing" and preparation can be great fun and often add to our sense of joyful anticipation. It can also feel quite scary to be the one responsible for ensuring that all our baby's needs will be met when he or she is born.

As with packing a suitcase, different people will have different ideas about what is important. For some, being ready might mean ticking off a checklist and planning everything down to the last detail. For others, being ready means shying away from things like "must-dos" and lists and simply taking things as they come. Take a moment to think about how you usually approach a time of preparation.

Are you a list maker? Do you thrive in chaos and adapt to whatever a situation throws at you, or do you like to know what to expect and plan accordingly? Do you usually leave preparations until the last minute, or do you need to have all your ducks in a row way ahead of time? And does your approach to preparation work for you? Are there any aspects that you would like to change?

These questions prove pertinent for many areas of our lives because, if you think about it, we spend most of our lives preparing for various events. The duration of an anticipated event is usually shorter than the time spent in preparation. For example, the time spent planning a trip is usually much longer than the trip itself! Do you remember all the days you spent studying for an exam, which was then over in one session? Or the months you spent preparing for your wedding that was over in just a few hours? We spend the nine months of pregnancy anticipating the birth of our baby—and the birthing will be over in a fraction of that time!

But what if we viewed pregnancy as a time of preparation for motherhood, rather than as a time of preparation for a birth? Our starting point in writing this book was that pregnancy offers us a valuable opportunity to take stock and prepare ourselves spiritually and emotionally for the life change that we will experience with our transition into motherhood. This whole book has been about preparation for the adventure ahead. Were you aware that as you read this book and responded to the reflection questions and invitations to prayer, you were already busy with the work of preparation for motherhood?

Each chapter has invited you, in some way, to prepare for the birth of your baby as well as to undergo a birthing within yourself. You've been encouraged to prepare for the new by releasing the way things were; you have participated in what God desires by embracing truth, facing fear, waiting and resting, and walking closely with God as you move toward wholeness. You also have opened yourself to enjoying the support of others during this time.

The next step we invite you to take is to embrace the change that is fast approaching. In this chapter we focus specifically on preparing ourselves emotionally, spiritually, and in practical ways to receive our baby through the process of birth and to welcome him or her into our hearts, lives, and homes. We also look at how God uses times of preparation in our lives.

Reflection

Take some time to page through this book again and reflect on some of the helpful steps, practical suggestions, and spiritual challenges that have meant something to you. Consider these in the light of your final preparations.

Preparing with God

> You prepare a table before me
> > in the presence of my enemies.
> You anoint my head with oil;
> > my cup overflows.
> > > —Psalm 23:5, NIV

Isn't it amazing that even God prepares? Jesus promises his disciples—and that includes us—that when he is in his Father's house, he will prepare a special place for us (John 14:2). Jesus is there even now, so can you guess what he is doing—preparing! And much as we would like to imagine what this place will look like, we cannot: "No eye has seen, no ear has heard, no mind has conceived what God has prepared for those who love him" (1 Cor. 2:9, NIV).

It is humbling to know that God, the creator and savior of the world, sees us as so important that God will put effort, thought, and planning into preparing a place for us. What does it mean to you to know that there is a unique place in God's heart and house for you?

But God is not the only one preparing. As God's people, we also prepare for God. Isaiah prophesied that there would be a voice calling, "In the desert prepare the way for the LORD; make straight in the wilderness a highway for our God" (Isa. 40:3, NIV). John the Baptist was the "voice" who prepared the way for Jesus, bringing a message that opened the minds and hearts of the Israelites to receive Jesus' message of forgiveness and freedom.

God uses times of preparation to work in our lives. Consider the example of the Jewish people, who took forty years to go a relatively short distance from Egypt to the Promised Land. God needed to prepare them for the responsibilities and celebrations of life as a settled people, rather than as an enslaved one. They needed to learn to trust God and to discover the value of building a new community.

During our time of pregnancy, God works in us to prepare us in a similar way. It's a time when we can learn to trust more fully in God and to mature in our relationship with the Divine. We listen to

God's still, small voice and discover an inner strength that perhaps we didn't realize we had, an innate resource to handle new situations and make courageous decisions. We can also draw closer to the people God has given us to love and receive support from them.

In the busyness of our preparations for our baby, we can benefit from remembering that God is at work within us, preparing us as well.

Reflection

In what ways do you sense God preparing you for motherhood?

Preparing to Welcome Our Baby

> "Please enter—my house is your house, my joy is your joy, my sadness is your sadness, and my life is your life."
> —Henri J. M. Nouwen, *Reaching Out*[1]

Hospitality was one of the most important traditions of ancient people. In ancient cultures people were willing to share shelter, warmth, and food with strangers not just as a gift, or with the hope that they might receive similar gifts in times of need, but because God required it. They understood hospitality not only as a matter of survival but also as an expression of their spirituality.

We see this tradition demonstrated in Genesis 18:1-15, as Abraham welcomes three strangers to rest and be refreshed in his home. A generous host, Abraham goes out of his way to make his guests feel comfortable, unaware that he is offering hospitality to the Lord's messengers. It comes as a wonderful surprise when his guests share the news that Sarah will bear the child that he and Sarah had given up hope of ever having.

The idea that hospitality is an important expression of our spirituality may not be new to us. The writer of Hebrews invites us not to neglect "to show hospitality to strangers, for some who have done this have entertained angels without realizing it!" (Heb. 13:2, NLT). But what may be new is the idea that as mothers we are extending hospitality to our babies. Our babies are essentially strangers to us. Although they are closer to us than any other person, we have not seen their faces or discovered who they are and how they respond to the world. They are unique human beings that we have yet to meet.

This may not be a comfortable thought for you. Our perceptions of strangers are no longer as open and generous as in ancient times. As children we learn to be wary of strangers and the unknown, so we may prefer not to think of our precious babies as strangers, but it helps us to accept that our children are not miniversions of us. They do not belong to us in the same way we own property or other possessions. They are unique individuals loved and created by God who will grow and develop in their own way. Well-known Christian author Henri J. M. Nouwen put this into perspective when he said:

> Our children are our most important guests, who enter into our home, ask for careful attention, stay for a while and then leave to follow their own way. Children are strangers whom we have to get to know. They have their own style, their own rhythm and their own capacities for good and evil.[2]

As strangers we have yet to meet, as guests with whom we at first share our bodies and then also our hearts, homes, and lives, we offer our babies hospitality. We do this in many ways, but perhaps especially when we welcome them and when we give them space.

The word *welcome* comes from the Old English *wilcuma*, in which *wil* means "desire or pleasure," and *cuma* means "come." So the translated phrase would mean something like "one whose coming is desired and pleasing." The *Concise Oxford Dictionary* defines *welcome* as a greeting that means, "Know that your coming here gives pleasure." This is the greeting we can offer our babies. With this understanding of welcome, our attitude becomes one of an excited host anticipating the arrival of an honored guest. Through our thoughts, our actions, and even our words, we can let our babies know: "Your coming gives me great pleasure."

Recently, when Leigh approached the entrance of a retreat center, she was deeply struck by the word *WELCOME* carved in huge letters against a stone wall. It seemed to be more than just a warm greeting; it was an invitation. She felt as if she was being invited to "Come to Wellness," "Come to Be Well," and even to "Come to the Well." As we welcome our newborns, we too can extend these invitations. We offer ourselves, our families, and our homes as places of wellness for our babies. These become safe places that protect, heal, and nurture our children as they grow into adults who are equipped to face the challenges and joys of life. We also extend an invitation to them to come to the "Well of Living Water"—the refreshing, renewing, life-giving water that flows from our faith in Jesus Christ.

To be hospitable also means to provide a space for our guest. Our babies will need a physical space set aside for them in our homes, but they will also need us to make space in our lives for them. Time is a precious commodity in our fast-paced world, but our new guests pay no attention to this idea. Time is meant only for them, and they demand and expect as much of it as we can give! So we will need to release certain things in order to give our babies the gift of time.

We also need to make space for our babies in our hearts and minds. In working through this book, you have been doing just that. Of course, this is a work in progress that continues for as long as we are mothers. As our babies grow and change, we do too, and we make ongoing adjustments to the space we offer our children.

As we wonder what our babies will look like, what their first sounds will be, what sort of personalities they will have, we anticipate the arrival of a stranger. But this is not a stranger we fear or distrust, rather one we welcome with pleasure and delight. As parents we offer our children-guests the hospitality of our hearts and homes, providing a loving space in which they can become their God-given selves. But as with all guests, we give them the freedom to leave when they need to. In this way, you may find you have entertained angels unaware. You never know.

Reflection

What do you anticipate with delight as you think about welcoming your baby?

Preparing Our Home

> Home wasn't built in a day.
> —Jane Ace[3]

The anticipation of bringing a baby home often creates a new awareness in us of our home environment: our rooms, furniture, gardens, cars, and pets will also have to play host to our new guest. We may think about how we'll rearrange areas to suit the practicalities, safety, and comfort of ourselves and our baby. Preparing our home can be great fun, but it's actually more for us than for the baby!

Take the baby's room, for example. Francois and I spent months choosing paint, daubing stencils on walls, and rearranging countertops. However, Sinead was born in midwinter, so padding down a freezing hallway to the nursery at 2:00 a.m. wasn't an inviting prospect. We kept her in our room for a few months and eventually realized that our loft-roomed house was impractical; we moved before Sinead got to use her nursery. I often had to dismiss thoughts of the new owner splashing paint over the Noah's Ark stencils I'd so painstakingly done!

A small baby does not require any immediate, drastic changes to the home. The changes will happen gradually as our babies grow. Perhaps part of getting ready now is just to make peace with the idea that a year or eighteen months down the line, our homes may not look the same as they do now.

There are, however, some practical arrangements that can be helpful. I'm a person who thrives on strategy, so part of my planning entailed reorganizing rooms into convenient working areas and reading up on tips for a user-friendly environment. I didn't fully understand all the implications of bringing a baby home, but I also tried to prepare myself by anticipating my reactions to this possibly overwhelming situation. I assumed I would have little time and even less sleep, and I might not be as organized as I would like.

So, in my last months of pregnancy, I stocked up on frozen meals and ready-made canned and boxed foods. I also bought time-saving devices, like a clothes dryer and an answering machine, so that laundry wouldn't escalate and I could screen calls when I had time. I also thought about how I would react if and when friends and family offered help. I enjoyed anticipating and planning and found they helped me to relax—they were essential for my preparation.

One of my most important considerations during this time was whether I would continue pursuing my career, which required me to work outside the home. I wasn't sure I wanted a tiny baby in day care, so I had to think about other options. I felt that I could only make a final decision once the baby was born, so I had to think about what I'd do in that interim time while I weighed all my options.

Let's see how others prepared themselves:

> My preparation consisted of reading as much as possible. . . . I spoke to other moms and tried to remember things from their experiences. Rory and I had discussions about our reactions to the thought of becoming parents. . . . We prepared a baby's room and packed and repacked the clothing cupboards [dressers] to see that we had everything! We made sure that the hospital bag was ready.
>
> —Kim V.

> I don't think too much planning actually makes a difference. One can become very absorbed in the planning and preparation.

Even if I'd had all the wisdom, I don't think I would've been fully prepared for what I went through once my baby was there.

—Elize

When Kim visited a friend whose style of parenting she appreciated, she carried a notebook and jotted things down. My approach was similar as I collected ideas. I didn't end up using all of them, but the process was helpful.

What we do specifically to prepare isn't actually important. The value is in developing our own sense of readiness to welcome our babies. It's easy to be distracted by all the "must-haves" because we're bombarded with lists and requirements. As we explored in the chapter on "Recognizing Myths," we're often subtly manipulated to want to have everything in order to appear the "perfect parent." The same caution applies here: a newborn baby does not require every bit of equipment nor a layette that resembles a Versace line.

"Having everything" is relative; "being ready" is open to interpretation. Let's sift through the lists of so-called essentials and decide what we really need in order to feel prepared. The key to our sense of preparedness is feeling comfortable with our process of preparation.

Reflection

- What practical preparations are you busy with at the moment?
- How do you feel about your preparations?

Preparing for the Hospital

A hospital's a place where you go to be born.

—Overheard on a playground

My friend Connie was teaching when she had signs of labor at thirty weeks. She recalls: "The class was spurred into action by the horror on my face—they thought the baby was coming any minute! A staff member drove me to my obstetrician's office. To make matters worse, my husband was away on business. All I could think was that none of my hospital bags was ready!" Connie's labor turned out to be a false alarm, but when she shared this incident at our prenatal class, I probably wasn't the only one who went home (then thirty-two weeks pregnant) and got my bags ready!

My labor bag had all sorts of goodies: birthing paraphernalia, massage oils, snacks, and hot packs. My hospital-stay bag held extras, like friends' phone numbers, a notebook, and thank-you cards, and my going-home bag contained baby's outfits and my clothes. When I walked past the nursery and caught a glimpse of my bags, my heart skipped a beat—they were a vivid reminder that the time was drawing closer. I was busy with all the tangible things related to the birth—it made all the imaginings and dreams real. We were having a baby, and it would happen soon!

The process of considering what we need and what we'll do without is necessary, even if things change or turn out differently.

At thirty-eight weeks, we faced the possibility of a cesarean section. The obstetrician said that if nothing changed within a few days, natural birth wouldn't be an option. By the time we visited the doctor again a few days later, we had made peace with his recommendation and agreed to a spinal block procedure. I gazed at my labor bag with a pang: all those well-planned snacks and oils!

"Ah, well," Francois said, "let's take them out and have a picnic." So we did.

That's the nature of preparation. It takes into account the possibilities and maybes. The process of considering what we need and what we'll do without is necessary, even if things change or turn out differently. Preparation means constant reorganization and weighing the pros and cons, all of which contribute to our state of readiness. Again, it's not about *what* we do or don't do, neither is it about whether our preparations work out, but that in our planning, we make peace with our own sense of readiness.

Reflection

What is the most important thing you need to do to feel ready to welcome your baby?

Preparing with Rituals and Celebrations

> Baby showers have seemed to me to be quite uncivilized rituals—many of those I've attended have been nothing short of chaotic get-togethers with hysterical women dressing up the mom-to-be, forcing her to guess the content of the presents, and making her pay lewd forfeits like sipping orange juice from a potty. . . . Some showers are quite pleasant though, as was mine . . . it was a lovely surprise breakfast with my closest friends, who, in turn, plied me with gifts and good wishes.
>
> —Linda's pregnancy journal

We often mark life transitions with a ritual or celebration. For example, weddings mark the transition from singleness to marriage. Our cultural heritage plays a big role in determining what kinds of ceremonies or celebrations we will participate in during our pregnancy. You may be planning for a naming ceremony. People may give you gifts in specific colors depending on the gender of your baby (if you have chosen to find out) or give you no gifts at all if your culture considers gift-giving before the baby's birth to be bad luck.

One of the common pregnancy rituals in Western culture is the baby shower. In my mother's day it was known as the stork party, which alludes to that lovely myth that the stork delivers a baby dangling in a bandanna from its beak! A new variation on this theme is a "pamper party," especially for moms expecting a second or third child, where the gifts are more for the mom-to-be than for the baby.

Many of us attended baby showers before having one of our own. These celebrations are often for women only, but men may be included. Showers have their own rituals, which vary depending on our circle of friends and current trends. Usually the shower is a party where the mother-to-be receives gifts for her baby and oohing and aahing abounds! The intent is to provide and spoil the parents-to-be with both the necessities and sentimental items for a baby. It's also a time of fellowship and laughter that can give older moms an opportunity to share their stories—a truly special moment for us as pregnant women to be affirmed and encouraged.

Many rituals and celebrations center around belief systems and religion. Christians sometimes hold special gatherings in which they pray for the pregnant couple and bless them, or they plan celebrations, often coinciding with a baptism or dedication, where new parents are encouraged, godparents are named, and gifts are given. All these rituals and gatherings help mark an important event in our lives. These times serve as stopping points in our everyday lives when we draw near to the people who are important to us and will be important to our baby. They are also times when we turn to God with gratitude and draw strength and encouragement for the way ahead.

What kind of gathering or ritual would help you prepare for your baby's birth? How can you include your husband, friends, family, or other significant persons? It may be as simple as meeting with one other couple to pray for you and your baby as you head into the final weeks of your pregnancy. Or perhaps you feel like a prebirth "letting go" party to celebrate your release of the way things were and your embrace of all that lies ahead. However you choose to mark the transition, doing so can help you to make meaning of your experience and make peace with change.

Reflection

How does your culture usually mark or celebrate the experience of pregnancy and birth?

Preparing a Name

> If I have a son I will not name him Robert Redford and if I have a daughter I will not name her Dolly Parton. These are good names, but they're taken.
>
> —Chris Colin[4]

Shakespeare's Juliet uttered the words: "What's in a name? That which we call a rose / By any other name would smell as sweet." While I can understand why Juliet feels so strongly about this, I don't think I entirely agree with her reasoning. Our names not only identify and distinguish us from others—they speak of a culture, an ancestry, a heritage, and the considered choice of two parents. Sometimes they reflect the generation or time period in which we were born.

God began the tradition of choosing unique names by naming Adam, and throughout the Bible we see the importance of names: they reflected destiny, promise, and character. God often changed the names of people so their purposes would be fully realized; their new names represented a vision for them to grow into. Abram became Abraham (Father of Many Nations); Jacob (Deceiver) became Israel (Wrestled with God); Simon became Peter (Rock).

When the angel visited Mary, he told her what name to give her baby. Rather than following the Jewish tradition of giving family names, Mary was to call her son Jesus. This name, meaning "God saves," revealed Jesus' role and purpose.

Our names can reflect something of who we are, and they do have a special meaning to God, who says, "I have redeemed you; I have [called] you by name; you are mine" (Isa. 43:1, NIV). Names identify us, but they also proclaim our unique place in God's eyes.

Therefore, the choice of our baby's name matters to both God and us. Whether a name is unusual or conventional, it will be the name that a person will respond to for the rest of his or her life. Our choice of a name can reflect many things. We might want to continue a family name, but we may have to accept that this may mean our little ones end up being called something else. The women in my mother's family have a string of family names that trip up the tongue; my grandmother's name was Gesina Johanna Francina Cecilia, which was conveniently shortened to Sienie.

Choosing our baby's name has relevance to both God and ourselves.

We may want to choose a name with a special meaning. Many people of Greek and Cypriot origin are named for saints, and their name days (the days of particular saints) are celebrated with as much ceremony as their birthdays. To simplify your choice, you could follow the practice of a certain Ghanaian tribe that names people for the day on which they were born. For example, Koku is given to a child born on Wednesday, and Ami to someone born on Saturday.

Francois and I paged through a name book, and our tongues tripped over exotic names, while others had uncomfortable associations or reminders of awkward people. We wanted our baby's name to be prophetic and filled with purpose, something reflecting her heritage and that she'd be happy to live up to. My maiden name is Irish, and Francois' family name is French, so we chose names to reflect these ancestries. Because we'd waited a long time for a child and were grateful to God, we wanted her name to express this. We chose Sinead, an Irish name meaning "God provides/is gracious," and Celeste, a French name meaning "heavenly blessing."

Esther shares this:

I prayed to God for a baby girl. I promised him that this baby would belong to him and that I would make sure of that. God answered my prayers, and we were blessed with the gift of a baby girl. We were so thankful, we named her Refilwe, which means, "we were given what we asked for."

Choosing names is fun, and it is a privilege. May our children's names be a blessing that reflects all our hopes and prayers for them.

Reflection

- What names are you considering for your baby? Why are these particularly special to you?
- Thank God for your name. Thank God that your name is written in the palm of God's hand (see Isa. 49:16).

Preparing with Faith

> Love the LORD your God with all your heart, all your soul, and all your strength. . . . commit yourselves wholeheartedly to these commands. . . . Repeat them again and again to your children. Talk about them when you are at home and when you are away on a journey, when you are lying down and when you are getting up.
> —Deuteronomy 6:5-7, NLT

My parents, Francois, and I were traveling from Venice to the Amalfi Coast in Italy. As we packed, getting everything in our luggage proved to be a challenge. Closing my mother's suitcase was the greatest feat, requiring two grown men to sit on the suitcase lid. We strapped and reinforced the suitcase so its contents wouldn't spill out.

I think of faith as being similar to those straps that hold everything together. We need to encase and strengthen our preparations for our baby with faith. Faith surrounds and secures life's essentials.

How do we prepare in faith for the life-changing experience of parenthood? How do we develop the kind of faith that will hold everything together even when it feels like we're full to overflowing and spilling out the sides? Faith is both an attitude and an activity. It is something we know because of who God is, and it is something we do because the right actions strengthen and demonstrate our faith.

Luke 10:38-42 provides a wonderful example of the attitude of faith. Jesus is visiting his good friends Lazarus, Martha, and Mary in their home. Mary sits at Jesus' feet, listening to him teach. Through her quiet attentiveness, she exemplifies trust and devotion. She demonstrates focused dedication, making herself utterly present to all that Jesus can teach and give her. She displays an attitude of complete trust in God and of desire to know and do God's will rather than her own. Sue Monk Kidd calls this posture "attention of the heart."[5]

Mary's desire for God, her thirst for Jesus' teaching, and her longing to be in his presence overcome any fear she has of being the only woman in what is traditionally a man's domain. (At that time only men were allowed to be discipled by a rabbi; this is still true of Orthodox Jews.) In choosing to sit at Jesus' feet, Mary resists both her sister's expectations and her culture's demands.

In this vignette Mary teaches us that preparation means much more than worrying about everything that needs to be done. Jesus chastises Martha not for being busy but for being distracted by her worry "about many things." Preparation is not only about doing all the things we believe have to be done. It also is about centering ourselves in the presence of God, who enfolds all that has gone before, all that currently occupies us, and all our future plans.

A vital aspect of preparing well for our baby's coming is acknowledging that ultimately we rely on God for all our needs. We can trust in God's presence and guidance in every aspect of our preparation. We can learn to sit at the feet of the Divine in listening attentiveness with hearts that seek God. We will find peace in knowing that our lives are in God's hands.

Suzaan and Antoinette prepared for their babies with faith. This is how they described it:

With pregnancy came the realization that parenthood without God's guidance, without faith, would be very difficult. Having faith, practicing to trust his judgment, experiencing his direction in my life, is what makes things possible. One plans ahead and then life happens. In order to deal with that, I've had to walk close with God so that he will also be there in every aspect of parenting.

—Suzaan

Even though we experienced the terrible loss of our first child, we were always aware of God's presence. . . . We marveled at God's timing in our second pregnancy and grew closer to him. The most positive aspect of my pregnancy was the knowledge that God was in control.

—Antoinette

I mentioned earlier that faith is both an attitude and an activity. The key to active faith is to be busy with the right activity at the right time. The story of Mary and Martha upsets many women; if we are honest, we feel a lot of empathy for Martha. We recognize our own longing to sit quietly at the feet of Jesus, but the loads of laundry, the report that must be written, and the list of phone calls to return all demand our attention instead. In the midst of our "Martha moments" it may be helpful to hear Jesus' invitation to prioritize and focus on the "one thing" that is needed. When action is called for, we need to discern the most important thing to do at that moment rather than getting distracted by all that is urgent. Times of prayer and reflection, even in small doses, can help clarify this for us.

For centuries Christians have participated in various activities, called spiritual disciplines, which have built their faith. The spiritual disciplines include prayer, worship, reading God's Word, reflection, and fellowship with other believers. When we engage in these activities to whatever extent is possible for us, we strengthen our faith.

The spiritual disciplines seem to challenge us to move in three directions. First, there is a journey inward that involves prayer, reflection, fasting, and times of quiet and solitude. There is also an outward journey that involves service, justice, sharing our faith with others, and caring for our world. And finally there is a journey into community that involves relationship building, worship, mentorship, discussion, and support.

Through the stories, suggestions, reflection questions, and prayer exercises in this book, we have invited you to engage with each of these three journeys. Our preparation has therefore taken on a far wider perspective than just ourselves and our babies. The spiritual journey that we have shared has not simply been a preparation for having a baby or for motherhood. It is an ongoing journey that can strengthen and sustain us through life and through the many other changes we will encounter.

Reflection

- In your preparations, how have you been conscious of God's presence?
- To which spiritual disciplines have you been drawn during your pregnancy? How are you growing in those disciplines?

Invitation to Prayer

We have spoken a great deal in this book about the journey of pregnancy, and in this chapter Linda compared our preparation during pregnancy to packing a suitcase for a trip. It seems appropriate therefore, that in this time of prayer we invite you to take a physical journey that we hope will also be a spiritual one. We suggest that you go for a prayer walk.

Much like having a baby, a prayer walk requires preparation, but it also opens up the possibility of discovering new and unexpected treasures along the way. When we enter a different environment from our usual places of prayer, we open ourselves to God speaking to us in new ways. We allow God to use our senses, the beauty and wonder of creation, and the Spirit within us to guide our thoughts. In doing this we can receive fresh insights that God wants to speak into our hearts in preparation for what will be when we are mothers.

To prepare for your prayer walk, decide where, when, and for how long you would like to go. You could choose to walk in your garden, a local park, or a retreat center. Choose a place that has natural beauty and where you won't be disturbed. Plan to spend at least half an hour to an hour. You may also decide to begin and end in your baby's room or at your baby's crib, or you might prefer to hold an item of baby clothing while you walk.

A walk in nature in an attitude of prayer and contemplation can be restful, refreshing, and invigorating. Therefore, take your prayer walk without any particular agenda. The purpose of this prayer walk is not to intercede for others, to question God, or to work through some issue. You can do all of these things at another time in prayer. Rather, use the prayer walk as an opportunity to listen to God.

As you begin your walk, you could ask God to guide you, speak to you, and fill you with a sense of God's abiding presence. You might say something like this:

> Dearest Lord, I ask that you will prepare my heart, soul, spirit, and body to receive what I need from you as I go on this walk. Open all my senses that I may be attentive and aware of how you wish to speak to me through your creation. I trust that your gentle presence will be with me, guiding and directing my steps on this simple journey, just as you will be guiding and directing my steps throughout my pregnancy, the birth of my baby, and my journey through motherhood. Amen.

During your walk, move slowly. You are not walking for exercise but for prayer. Stop as soon as something captures your attention. It may be an insect, a flower, a moss-covered rock. We often complain about not having time to "smell the roses"; now is that time! Use all your senses to see colors, shapes, designs; hear whirring bees' wings and bird chirps; smell flowers and freshly cut grass; and feel the texture of leaves, bark, rough and smooth stones. You may wish to remove your shoes and feel the grass under your feet or the warm sun on the stone path. You may like to lie on your back and watch the clouds waft across the sky.

Now take some time to reflect on the particular things that caught your attention. Why do they seem important for you right now? What do they say to you about God, about your baby, about your preparations for his or her birth? Listen also for what God may be saying to you. How does this help you to feel better prepared for what lies ahead? Spend some time thanking God for giving you what you need on this journey.

When you are ready, you may want to write about your experience in your journal. In this way you keep the memory fresh and available for whenever you need to be reminded that God is with you and you do not face the future alone.

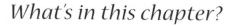

What's in this chapter?

*B*irth is both an ending and a beginning as we embark on a new journey with our newborn baby. We give birth, and we are birthed into a new role and a new responsibility as we become mothers.

- Releasing our babies from our wombs
- Birthing
- Being birthed
- Invitation to Prayer: Write a letter of blessing and encouragement to your baby

11

I'M A MOTHER!

Of all the joys that lighten suffering earth, what joy is welcomed like a new-born child?

—Caroline Norton

Linda...

Scheduled for a cesarean section, I had gone into the hospital the evening before the procedure. It was a sleepless night because I was uncomfortable in a strange bed, with the staff coming at odd intervals to monitor my baby's heartbeat. In the early hours of the morning, someone nearby went into labor. By dawn, I'd felt as though I'd run a hundred miles. It did little to mar the day; it was the day of my baby's birth!

Here is an extract from the letter I wrote to Sinead on the day of her birth:

> Even though we knew that your coming was today, we weren't anxious or nervous—we had peace and a sense of anticipation that was quiet and inevitable. . . .The [operating room] was hyper-organized and clinical with bright lights overhead, beeping machinery, and fussing professionals. The air was filled with

jovial bantering, the atmosphere relaxed, and I felt my lower body numbing. . . . within minutes your presence was made known . . .

Voices said, "A girl!" and the obstetrician leaned over and said, "Congratulations, Mommy, you have a lovely little girl," and we heard your loud cries as they lifted you up, and both Dad and I were dumbstruck as we gazed at your writhing body and howling face. . . . (I thought: "You don't look like anyone I know") . . . you and Dad left with the pediatrician, and I lay in a kind of daze while being stitched up.

My initial reactions were quite euphoric: my thanks to the doctors, my saying the baby's name for the first time. Francois and I were alone for a few moments in the ward because Sinead had been placed in an incubator, and it was like being in a vacuum—we tried to relive the past two hours with our jumbled recollections and sharply etched impressions (which would have to do, because Francois had forgotten to take photographs!). When Sinead was brought in, we pored over her, thanked God, and were quite overcome.

A few things stand out in my memories of that day: we were in shock as we phoned people to tell the news; our emotions hadn't caught up with events. We had not experienced hours of labor; the C-section had been very quick, and we were still trying to come to terms with the fact that the birthing was over.

The visiting hour was a blur: it was a cacophony of shrill reactions, an explosion of pink carnations, and a confetti of good wishes while Sinead lay in the nursery with everyone pointing through the glass. That night I gratefully succumbed to a sedated state while trying to come to grips with the reality of my baby's existence. I had no idea how irreversible a new baby's presence would be or how I'd change as a person. All I thought was, *She's finally here; I've wanted her so much, and she's everything I've longed for.*

Birth is both a culmination and beginning. A culmination because it is the end of the trimesters of pregnancy and of waiting. It is a journey in which we've experienced our baby's development, the changes in our bodies, and all the preparations we've been busy with. These parts are over; we have reached a destination.

We also face new beginnings. It is the beginning of our baby's life and the start of our roles as parents. We're beginning to get to know this new human being. We're beginning to taste the responsibilities of caring and providing for our baby. We're embarking on a new journey.

Reflection

- As you stand on the threshold of giving birth, what would you consider as endings for you?
- What beginnings do you anticipate?

Releasing Our Babies from Our Wombs

> Every time the mother takes a breath, the baby is slightly rocked. When the mother coughs, when she laughs, when she walks, there is a commotion in the baby's pool of fluids and the baby is swayed back and forth. The effect of a mother lightly dancing is different from a mother striding down the street.
> —Geraldine Lux Flanagan, *Beginning Life*[1]

No closer physical bond exists between two people than that of a mother to the baby in her womb. Mother and child share blood, nutrients, and body space. A mother can literally say of her child that he is flesh of her flesh. This is how Corine expressed it: "I enjoyed the feeling of, 'Baby, wherever I go, you go. We're in this together!'"

We provide a nurturing, protective environment for our baby in utero. But our baby also shares community with us. We have the delight of the baby's companionship and movement, growth and unconditional acceptance of us for the nine months of our pregnancy. Once our baby is born, personality differences, generational differences, and life experiences all serve to separate us from that initial connection we had with our child. This is part of the natural course of life. Our children will become their own persons, independent from us, and able to make their own choices in life. This is our job as parents—to guide them as best we can to make their own way in the world as confident, caring individuals.

Some mothers feel sad at the thought of letting go the intimacy of carrying their baby within their bodies. God must have seen this coming and ensured that we would be so uncomfortable by the end of the nine months that we would release our babies quite willingly to the birth process! Many mothers also describe a growing desire, even an aching toward the end of pregnancy, to hold their babies in their arms, touch their soft cheeks, and stroke their downy hair.

The intensity of connection we have with our baby during pregnancy may not last, but the wonder of having experienced this gift and the desire to nurture our connection with our children does endure, and for this we are grateful.

Reflection

What do you enjoy most about the bond you share with your baby while you are so intimately connected?

Birthing

> There is nothing on earth like the moment of seeing one's first baby. [People] scale other heights, but there is no height like this simple one, occurring continuously throughout the ages in musty bedrooms, in palaces, in caves and desert places. I looked at this rolled-up bundle . . . and knew again I had not created her. . . . She had her own life to lead, her own destiny to accomplish; she just came past me to this earth.
>
> —Katharine Trevelyan[2]

How does one describe the experience of giving birth? It's different for everybody. As Naomi Wolf says, "When I finally gave birth, nothing happened the way I had imagined."[3]

Each birth is a unique event, always our own unparalleled, "lived-through" moment. Kim and Leigh share their stories:

> Within half an hour of my water breaking, the contractions were two minutes apart and I was now officially terrified. We had a twenty-minute drive to the hospital, and I was convinced that my baby would be born in the car. I refused to leave home. . . . I'd rather the baby be born at home than next to the highway in morning rush hour. . . . Dave coaxed me into the car.
>
> Suddenly I realized that in an upright position, gravity was on my baby's side. I squeezed to the backseat. "What you doing?" said a panicking Dave, thinking I was trying to escape. "I'm crouching down with my butt in the air," I gasped. "That way, the baby can't come out." I breathed, prayed, and navigated all the way to the hospital. We screeched into the hospital grounds. . . . a wheelchair appeared, and I was whisked up to the birthing unit. . . . Dave forgot the labor bag in the car, so there wasn't music, candles, or massage oils. . . . Then there was a warm, wet, wriggling little person on my chest, and time was suspended.
>
> —Kim

> I'd heard of women screaming, swearing, and almost going wild in the midst of labor, and I feared that I would lose control in a similar way. I spent the morning walking as intense pain gripped me in spasms in my lower back. My husband tried massaging me, which only irritated me. He got on with work while I paced and winced. He seemed detached, and yet what else could he do? Eventually I was put on a drip to induce stronger contractions. Later, a midwife came to help, and I managed to get this new little being into the world.
>
> —Leigh

You have probably heard countless birthing stories during your pregnancy, and each one is unique. Some are awful and others are wonderful, and we have no way of knowing in advance which ours will be. We need to be careful that the myth of perfectionism doesn't sneak into our ideas about the kind of birth experience we would like to have. Let's dispel the myth right now: there is no such thing as a perfect birth—for one thing, it would be just about impossible to get two people to agree on what it would look like or be like! And no single birth option is objectively better than another. We can only make a reasoned decision based on our own unique circumstances.

Unfortunately, judgment and criticism abound when it comes to discussing birth options, often leaving women feeling inadequate or angry. Actress Kate Winslet admits that she lied for two years about her "wonderful" natural birth experience with her first child, when in fact she had to have an emergency cesarean section. She says that she felt like a failure after her ideal birthing experience did not materialize, and she couldn't face people knowing.

Perfectionist ideals are not simply unreasonable—they are destructive and rob us of joy and freedom. Heather, Leigh, and Kim V. share this:

> I elected to have a cesarean and was treated as an "odd bod." I remember a prenatal class where couples discussed their thoughts on birth. I was stunned to hear how anticesarean they all were. Thankfully, by the time they got to me, the conversation was so sidetracked, I managed to wheedle my way out. That experience will stick in my mind forever.
>
> —Heather

> For years, I struggled with a sense of failure. I berated myself for not getting into the right position, that I hadn't pushed hard enough, that all those prenatal classes had counted for nothing. I had a beautiful little girl, but a nagging thought persisted: I was disappointed in my "performance." God has had to do a healing work in me. I look back on my labor experience with awe, gratitude, and celebration. We do ourselves a disservice when we are so unkind to ourselves.
>
> —Leigh

We're caught up with all the aspects of pregnancy and birth—there are so many choices for childbirth. It's all about whether we want "natural" childbirth, a cesarean, drugs or not, hospital or home, epidurals, episiotomies, etc. These seem like such big decisions, but when all is said and done and the baby's in your arms, that's when the "real" stuff starts. I think we create unnecessary stress for ourselves, worrying about things that we should or shouldn't be doing.

—Kim V.

As you anticipate labor and birth, remember two important things. First, you are having a baby rather than a birth experience, and while birthing can only go on for a limited period of time, your baby will be with you forever. Second, you do not face giving birth alone. Whatever your experience of birth, God will be there and God's loving presence is like a deep well that you can draw strength and courage from during labor. In "Encountering God" we considered the image of God as our birth companion or midwife. God accompanies us during our pregnancy and therefore will also be present at the birth—supporting us and guiding our baby into the world.

Let's allow ourselves the grace to accept the varied challenges that birthing brings. Let us trust in our ability to remain flexible and make any necessary adjustments, so that we can participate fully in the wonder of the birthing experience. However it happens, childbirth remains an overwhelming, miraculous event—when the glorious moment arrives, we will participate with God in bringing forth new life.

A baby represents so many things! Here, mere moments after birth, a baby epitomizes the newness of life. Every day will be a milestone, every month a new phase of development, and every year a stepping-stone. This baby is embarking on the great adventure of life, and we have the privilege of experiencing with our child all the wonders that she or he will encounter for the first time: stars against a black sky, a lemon's zest, a crawling ladybug.

As we hold our babies in our arms, they offer us new hope—the hope of new life and all the wonder and joy that life holds. Babies are also a sign of hope in the future, the future of our family, the future of our community and world. Each one has a unique role to play in furthering God's kingdom. As we have carried these babies within us, we have carried the seeds of that hope, and now we offer this hope to the world.

Reflection

- What expectations do you have regarding the birthing experience?
- What would it mean to you to lay them aside, if need be?

Being Birthed

[Birth is] the sudden opening of a window through which you look out upon a stupendous prospect. For what has happened? A miracle. You have exchanged nothing for the possibility of everything.

—William M. Dixon[4]

The world is new not only for our baby but also for us. Our lives will take on new dimensions and disciplines. We will experience ourselves, others, and God in a new way—that is the promise of birth!

It is impossible to predict how we will feel just after giving birth. The popular image is of being overcome with a sudden rush of emotion and an immediate connection with our babies. Many women do experience this. Many have a sense of indescribable love and protection or overwhelming feelings of elation. Others are suddenly confronted with unanticipated disconnection and/or anxiety, and these emotions can be bewildering.

Think about it: we have just undergone a tumultuous experience. It is no small feat to participate in the giving of life. It has taken all our resources of body, mind, and spirit to engage in labor and childbirth—and it will take everything in our body, mind, and spirit to recover fully. At any other time, if our bodies have undergone any trauma or surgical intervention, we usually understand the need for physical recuperation. So it is with the birthing experience. We also need to allow our emotions the space to recover. We may need a little time to come to terms with what's happened to us.

It is important at this point to acknowledge the courage it takes to have come this far. Taking on the responsibility to carry full term and give birth are not flimsy choices. We have had to learn, grow, and change—courageous decisions, bravely borne. Naomi Wolf says:

> The joy of a new child . . . does not do away with the reality of the tough journey we as mothers undertake. We do not so much fall into motherhood as forge ourselves into mothers. . . .
>
> The tough journey and the happy ending are both part of the truth of pregnancy; just as they are part of the truth of motherhood. It is no dilution of our great love for our children to honour the effort that women make.[5]

Through the tough journey of birthing we have changed as well, and we emerge from the experience as a person with a new role, a new task, and a new responsibility. The thought that we have become someone that another being now looks up to can be quite intimidating. Suddenly we're the person who needs to provide nourishment, protection, and constant care. While others congratulate and playfully call us "mommy," there is a real little person whose mommy we are and whose wants and needs depend on our provision and love. And, despite our careful preparation, we may have missed a few essential lessons!

Sinead had been with me a few hours when I became aware that she needed a diaper change. Changing a diaper had always seemed pretty straightforward, but now I realized that I had no idea which end of the diaper went where, and if I wanted my baby to stop squalling, I'd better look the part quickly! I pressed the bell for the nurse; when I explained I didn't know how to change a diaper, she stared incredulously. So I said, "You mean we're all born knowing how to do this?" She did a slow, deliberate demonstration that made me feel like a preschooler!

Becoming a mother overnight is literally true; making the powerful transition into motherhood takes a little longer. I knew in theory that life would change, but I had no idea how challenging motherhood would be. It was the beginning of a journey into an unknown place—of indescribable joys, vexing frustration, and unfathomable love. There were facets to my personality I was yet to meet: some frightening and some incredibly tender. I am continually being birthed into the mother that God intended me to be.

God has set us on a path, the path of parenthood, with the promise never to leave us or forsake us.

God has set us on a path, the path of parenthood, with the promise never to leave us or forsake us. It will be God's parent-heart that we'll tap into, and that will be our strength as we journey on. We may be excited or uncertain, but we will never be alone.

We have journeyed a long way together through the pages of this book. And what an awesome journey it has been—with ourselves, with others, and, always, with God. What a privilege it has been to companion you during this holy and precious time. It is our deepest prayer that you have encountered the grace and gentleness of God through these pages and that you face motherhood with a fresh and lasting awareness of your belovedness. We encourage you to draw out anything you have found to be of value: perhaps a particular insight, practice, or an approach to prayer, and to build it into your daily life as you journey on.

Reflection

What is the most important thing that has become clear to you during your pregnancy that you would like to take with you as your journey into motherhood continues?

Invitation to Prayer

As your due date comes closer and you begin to anticipate the thrill of holding your baby in your arms, we invite you to spend some time in prayer, writing a letter to your baby. It will be the kind of letter you might want to give when your child is old enough, at a time when he needs a word of love and encouragement from Mom, or when the world has given her a hard time and she needs a reminder that from the very beginning she was loved and welcomed.

Knowing how and where to start with such a letter can be more difficult than you think. It may help to look at a letter in scripture, one that Paul wrote to Timothy, the son of his heart. The letter is recorded in 2 Timothy 1:1-7.

Paul begins his letter by declaring who he is. As you have journeyed through this book and through your pregnancy, what have you learned about yourself? What insights do you want to share with your baby about who you are, where you have come from, and what holds you together? Perhaps use this time to look through your journal and underline or write out what you have learned and gained over this time. What in particular would you like to share with your baby?

Then Paul gives Timothy a blessing: "Grace, mercy and peace from God the Father and Christ Jesus our Lord" (2 Tim. 1:2, NIV). With what blessing do you want to greet your baby? How do you want your child to experience God in her life? What picture of God do you want your child to hold on to?

Next, Paul tells Timothy that he constantly remembers him in his prayers. What are your prayers for your baby? What requests have you made of God already?

Paul writes, "I long to see you, so that I may be filled with joy" (2 Tim. 1:4, NIV). Perhaps this is how you feel about your baby's arrival. Describe your thoughts and feelings at this point, and tell your baby about the preparations you have been making for him, your special guest.

Then Paul speaks of Timothy's family and heritage. Tell your baby who else anticipates his or her arrival. Who are the people your baby will meet? Whose arms will hold your child when he or she is first born? Who shares your excitement and anticipation?

Finally, Paul says, "I remind you to fan into flame the gift of God, which is in you through the laying on of my hands. For God did not give us a spirit of timidity, but a spirit of power, of love and of self-discipline" (2 Tim. 1:6-7, NIV). What better words to leave with your child! Acknowledge that God has gifted your child, and encourage her to use the gifts God has given her to serve the world. Assure him that God's Spirit will equip him with whatever he needs on his journey through life. What other words of encouragement and assurance do you want to give to your baby?

Paul ends his letter by saying, "The Lord be with your spirit. Grace be with you" (2 Tim. 4:22, NIV). How do you want to end your letter? What final blessing do you want to leave with your baby?

We also leave you with a blessing as you enter into motherhood:

The LORD bless you and keep you;
the LORD make his face shine upon you
    and be gracious to you;
the LORD turn his face toward you
    and give you peace.

—Numbers 6:24-26, NIV

NOTES

CHAPTER 1: I'M PREGNANT!

Epigraph. George MacDonald, *At the Back of the North Wind* (Uhrichsville, OH: Barbour Publishing, 2005), 271.

1. Elizabeth Stone, quoted in *The Best of Women's Quotations*, ed. Helen Exley (New York: Exley, 1993), 18.

2. Elizabeth Lesser, *Broken Open: How Difficult Times Can Help Us Grow* (New York: Random House, 2005), 237.

3. Lewis Thomas, *The Medusa and the Snail* (London: Allen Lane, 1980), quoted in Paul Brand and Philip Yancey, *Fearfully and Wonderfully Made* (London: Hodder and Stoughton, 1980), 25.

4. Margaret Hebblethwaite, *Motherhood and God*, 2nd ed. (London: Geoffrey Chapman Publishers, 1994).

CHAPTER 2: LISTENING TO OUR STORIES

Epigraph. Thomas Merton, *The Intimate Merton: His Life from His Journals*, eds. Patrick Hart and Jonathan Montaldo (Oxford: Lion Publishing, 2002), July 17, 1956 entry, 146–47.

1. Jim and Heather Johnston led the Life Revision course at Beth Shalam Retreat Centre in Hilton, Kwa-Zulu Natal, South Africa.

2. With gratitude to Michael White, who first spoke about the possibility of "saying hello again" to those we have lost, rather than "letting go" of them.

3. Muriel Rukeyser, "The Speed of Darkness," in *The Speed of Darkness* (New York: Random House, 1968), stanza 9, lines 3–4.

4. Subir Bhaumik, "Tsunami Folklore 'Saved Islanders,'" BBC News, http://news.bbc.co.uk/2/hi/south_asia/4181855.stm.

5. Michael White, *Re-Authoring Lives: Interviews and Essays* (Adelaide, South Australia: Dulwich Centre Publications, 1995), 83.

6. Alice Morgan, *What Is Narrative Therapy?: An Easy-to-Read Introduction* (Adelaide, South Australia: Dulwich Centre Publications, 2000), 5.

7. Trevor Hudson, *Signposts to Spirituality* (Cape Town: Struik Christian Books, 1995), 34.

8. Parker J. Palmer, *Let Your Life Speak: Listening for the Voice of Vocation* (San Francisco: Jossey-Bass, 2000), 3.

9. Ibid., 6–7.

10. Anne Lamott, *Traveling Mercies: Some Thoughts on Faith* (New York: Anchor Books, 2000), 213.

11. Margaret Silf, *Taste and See: Adventuring into Prayer* (London: Darton, Longman & Todd, 1999), 56.

12. Frederick Buechner, *Telling Secrets* (San Francisco: HarperSanFrancisco, 1991), 30.

13. Margaret Silf, *Landmarks: An Ignatian Journey* (London: Darton, Longman & Todd, 1998), 53.

14. Anne Long, *Listening* (London: Darton, Longman & Todd, 1990), 4–5.

15. Silf, *Taste and See*, 54.

16. Søren Kierkegaard, *The Diary of Søren Kierkegaard*, ed. Peter P. Rohde (New York: Carol Publishing Group, 1993), 111.

CHAPTER 3: RELEASING THE WAY THINGS WERE

Epigraph. Harriet Lerner, *The Mother Dance: How Children Change Your Life* (London: Thorsons/HarperCollins, 1999), 9.

1. Ibid., 8.

2. Trevor Hudson, *The Serenity Prayer: A Simple Prayer to Enrich Your Life* (Cape Town: Struik Christian Books, 2002), 26.

3. Flora Slosson Wuellner, *Prayer and Our Bodies* (Nashville: The Upper Room, 1987), 59.

4. Naomi Wolf, *Misconceptions: Truth, Lies, and the Unexpected on the Journey to Motherhood* (London: Chatto and Windus, 2001), 56.

5. Jan L. Richardson, *Sacred Journeys: A Woman's Book of Daily Prayer* (Nashville: Upper Room Books, 1995), 35.

6. Sue Monk Kidd, *When the Heart Waits: Spiritual Direction for Life's Sacred Questions* (San Francisco: HarperSanFrancisco, 1992), 4.

CHAPTER 4: RECOGNIZING MYTHS

Epigraph. John F. Kennedy, quoted in Aminatta Forna, *Mother of All Myths: How Society Moulds and Constrains Mothers* (London: HarperCollins Publishers, 1998), 259.

1. Stanislaw, in *Webster's New World Dictionary of Quotable Definitions*, 2nd ed., ed. Eugene E. Brussell (Englewood Cliffs, NJ: Prentice Hall, 1988), 384.

2. Wolf, *Misconceptions*, 53.

3. Forna, *Mother of All Myths*, 88.

4. Louis Fontanes, in *Webster's New World Dictionary of Quotable Definitions*, 423.

CHAPTER 5: FACING FEAR

1. Palmer, *Let Your Life Speak*, 18.

2. See Heidi Murkoff, Arlene Eisenberg, and Sandee Hathaway, *What to Expect When You're Expecting*, 3rd ed. (New York: Workman, 2002), xv–xvi.

3. Hebblethwaite, *Motherhood and God*.

4. Grace Sheppard, *An Aspect of Fear* (London: Darton, Longman & Todd, 1989), 30.

5. See Trevor Hudson with Morton Kelsey, *Journey of the Spirit: Devotions for the Spiritual Seeker* (Cape Town: Struik Christian Books, 2000), Week 25.

6. Katherine Paterson, *Jacob Have I Loved* (New York: HarperCollins, 1980), 50.

7. Sheppard, *An Aspect of Fear*, 34.

8. Ibid., 54.

9. Henri J. M. Nouwen, *The Inner Voice of Love: A Journey through Anguish to Freedom* (London: Darton, Longman & Todd, 1997), 41.

10. See Hudson, "Acknowledging Our Shadow Selves," in *Signposts to Spirituality*, 59–69.

11. Ibid., 60.

12. Frederick Buechner, *Telling Secrets*, 2–3.

13. With deep appreciation to Henri J. M. Nouwen, *Bread for the Journey: Reflections for Every Day of the Year* (London: Darton, Longman and Todd, 1996),

12, for his helpful ideas on fruitfulness and success.

14. Silf, *Taste and See*, 201.

15. Nouwen, *Bread for the Journey*, 21.

16. Henri J. M. Nouwen, *Life of the Beloved: Spiritual Living in a Secular World* (New York: Crossroad Publishing Company, 1992), 31.

17. Mark Twain, *The American Claimant* (Project Gutenberg, 2006), chap. 15, http://www.gutenberg.org/files/3179/3179.txt.

18. Mary Anne Radmacher, writer and artist, quote accessed at Thinkexist.com under the author's name.

19. Erica Jong, in *The Writer on Her Work,* ed. Janet Sternburg (New York: W. W. Norton & Company, 1980).

20. Sheppard, *An Aspect of Fear*, 65.

CHAPTER 6: ENCOUNTERING GOD

Epigraph. Richardson, *Sacred Journeys*, 284.

1. Joanne Sanders, "A Life of Pilgrimage: A Reflection for Alumni Weekend,"http://stanford.edu/group/religiouslife/docs/sermons/2003/sermon_10-19-2003_Sanders.pdf.

2. Francis Thompson, "The Hound of Heaven," in *The Oxford Book of Mystical Verse*, ed. D. H. S. Nicholson and A. H. E. Lee (Oxford: Clarendon Press, 1917), http://www.bartleby.com/236/239.html.

3. Richardson, *Sacred Journeys*, 254–55.

4. Flora Slosson Wuellner, *Heart of Healing, Heart of Light: Encountering God Who Shares and Heals Our Pain* (Nashville: Upper Room Books, 1992), 21.

5. Richardson, *Sacred Journeys*, 49.

6. Helen Exley, ed., *To the World's Best Mother* (Mount Kisco, NY: Exley Giftbooks, 1992), n.p.

7. Francis MacNutt, *Healing* (London: Hodder and Stoughton, 1988), 55.

8. Lerner, *The Mother Dance*, 8.

9. Richardson, *Sacred Journeys*, 253.

CHAPTER 7: BECOMING WHOLE

Epigraph. Kidd, *When the Heart Waits*, 4.

1. Wuellner, *Prayer and Our Bodies*, 31.

2. Joyce Rupp, *Your Sorrow Is My Sorrow: Hope and Strength in Times of Suffering* (New York: Crossroad Publishing Company, 1999), 98.

3. Jim Johnston and his wife, Heather, run Beth Shalam Retreat Centre in Hilton, Kwa-Zulu Natal, South Africa. This statement was part of the input Jim provided when my husband and I attended a Life Revision course there in 1999.

4. Henri J. M. Nouwen, *Reaching Out: The Three Movements of the Spiritual Life* (New York: Image Books, 1986), 35.

5. Jenna du Prees, "My Mother, My Self," in *O, The Oprah Magazine* (May 2004): 132–33.

6. Helen Keller, quoted in: http://www.journeyofhearts.org/transition/quotes_tr.html.

7. Wuellner, *Prayer and Our Bodies*, 31.

8. Ibid., 43.

9. Quote by Ernest Hemingway: "The world breaks everyone and afterward many are strong at the broken places," in *A Farewell to Arms* (New York: Scribner Paperback Fiction, 1995), 249.

10. Carl G. Jung, "The Symbolic Life" (seminar talk, Guild for Pastoral Psychology, London, 1939), http://www.jung.org/readingcorner.html.

11. Pema Chödrön, *Start Where You Are: A Guide to Compassionate Living* (Boston: Shambhala, 2001), x.

12. Marjorie J. Thompson, "Moving Toward Forgiveness," in *Weavings* 7, no. 2 (March/April 1992):21.

13. The story of the prodigal son, a parable Jesus told, is recorded in Luke 15:11-32.

14. Nancy Good Sider, "At the Fork in the Road: Trauma Healing," Journey toward Forgiveness Web site: http://www.journeytowardforgiveness.com/mapping/article1.asp, 4.

15. Thanks to Vanessa Michael for introducing me to this beautiful idea.

CHAPTER 8: WAITING

Epigraph. Simone Weil, *The Simone Weil Reader*, ed. George A. Panichas (Wakefield, RI: Moyer Bell, 1977), 438.

1. http://people.msoe.edu/~taylor/humor/sw_fake.htm and http://www.wright-house.com/steven-wright/steven-wright-As.html.

2. Suzanne Mayer, "The Poverty of Waiting and Its Riches," *Spirituality Today* 42, no. 4 (Winter 1990): 292–302.

3. Nouwen, *Bread for the Journey*, 359.

4. Dennis Bratcher, "A Prayer of Hope: Verse Commentary on Isaiah 64:1-12," The Voice, CRI/Voice Institute Web site,
http://www.cresourcei.org/isa64.html.

5. See Ibid.

6. Nouwen, *Bread for the Journey*, 360.

7. Richard Rohr, "Everything Belongs," retreat held in Johannesburg, South Africa, June/July 2002. Rohr led the retreat; the theme was based on his book *Everything Belongs: The Gift of Contemplative Prayer* (New York: Crossroad Publishing Company, 1999).

8. Trevor Hudson's book *The Serenity Prayer* (Cape Town: Struik Christian Books, 2002), is a useful guide to journeying with this prayer.

9. With deep appreciation to Gail Jupp, who taught so many through her words and her example, to "celebrate the little things."

10. Palmer, *Let Your Life Speak*, 30–31.

11. George Matheson, "O Love That Wilt Not Let Me Go," in *The United Methodist Hymnal* (Nashville: United Methodist Publishing House, 1989), no. 480.

12. Kidd, *When the Heart Waits*, 13.

13. Ibid., 14.

14. Ibid., 22.

CHAPTER 9: EMBRACING OTHERS

Epigraph. Larry Crabb, *Connecting: Healing for Ourselves and Our Relationships, A Radical New Vision* (Nashville: Word Publishing, 1997), xix.

1. David Gottesman, American businessman, quote accessed on http://en.thinkexist.com/quotes/david_gottesman/.

2. "Preparing for Parenthood," *Your Pregnancy* (Winter 1999), 88.

3. Ibid.

4. Jo Boyden, *Families: Celebration and Hope in a World of Change* (Paris: UNESCO Publishing, 1993), 24.

5. Richardson, *Sacred Journeys*, 351.

6. Robert J. Wicks, *Touching the Holy: Ordinariness, Self-Esteem, and Friendship* (Notre Dame, IN: Ave Maria Press, 1992), 123.